Canadian Social Attitudes and Beliefs 1972-1997: A Select Bibliography

Compiled by

Shabiran Rahman
Dr. Ronald D. Lambert

Waterloo, Ontario
University of Waterloo Library

Canadian Social Attitudes and Beliefs 1972-1997: A Select Bibliography
Copyright ©1999 University of Waterloo Library

ISBN 0-920834-17-5

Produced by the University of Waterloo Library: Bibliography and Index produced with ProCite; final formatting completed in Microsoft Word.

Printed at Graphics, University of Waterloo.

Canadian Cataloguing in Publication Data

Rahman, Shabiran
  Canadian social attitudes and beliefs 1972-1997 : a select bibliography

(University of Waterloo Library bibliography ; no. 20)
Includes index.
ISBN 0-920834-17-5

1. Canadians – Attitudes – Bibliography. 2. Public opinion – Canada – Bibliography. 3. Canada – Social conditions – 1971-1991 – Public opinion – Bibliography. 4. Canada – Social conditions – 1991- - Public opinion – Bibliography. I. Lambert, Ronald D., 1936- . II. University of Waterloo. Library. III. Title. IV. Series.

Z7164.P956R33 1999   016.3033'8'0971   C99-931279-0

The following titles have been published in the bibliography series at the University of Waterloo Library:

No. 1   *Business: A Guide to Select Reference Sources*, 1978. O/P

No. 2   *Comparative Provincial Politics of Canada: A Bibliography of Select Periodical Articles, 1970-1977*, 1978. O/P

No. 3   *A Catalogue of the Dance Collection in the Doris Lewis Rare Book Room, University of Waterloo Library*, 1979. O/P

No. 4   *Terrorism: 1970-1978*, 1979. O/P

No. 5   *A Catalogue of the Library of George Santayana in the University of Waterloo Library*, 1980. O/P

No. 6   *Aspects of Negotiations between States*, 1981. O/P

No. 7   *A Catalogue of the Lady Aberdeen Library on the History of Women in the University of Waterloo Library*, 1982. O/P

No. 8   *Ralph Nader Bibliography 1960-1982*, 1982. O/P

No. 9   *A Guide to Research Collections in Microform in the Arts Library*, 1983. O/P

No. 10   *A Catalogue of the Dance Collection in the Doris Lewis Rare Book Room, University of Waterloo Library*. Second edition, revised and enlarged, 1983. O/P

No. 11   *A Guide to the John Herbert Papers in the University of Waterloo Library*, 1984. O/P

No. 12   *The Nature and Properties of Very Sensitive Clays: A Descriptive Bibliography*, 1985. O/P

No. 13   *Lucy Maud Montgomery: A Preliminary Bibliography*, 1986. O/P

No. 14   *Strategic Minerals: A Bibliography*, 1987. O/P

No. 15   *Isabel Ecclestone Mackay Bibliography*, 1987. O/P

No. 16   *Contemporary Canadian Indian Statistics Published by the Federal Government - 1960-1985: A Selective Bibliography and Subject Index to Sources Available in the University of Waterloo Library*, 1987. O/P

No. 17   *Bibliography of Technical Reports in the Fields of Computer
           Science and Computer Engineering Issued at the University of
           Waterloo from 1967 to 1987*, 1988. O/P

No. 18   *Catalogue of the Bertram R. Davis "Robert Southey" Collection*,
           1990. $25.00.

No. 19   *Homelessness in Canada: A Selective Bibliography*, 1991.
           $10.00.

Order from: Davis Centre Library Office
                   University of Waterloo
                   Waterloo, Ontario, Canada N2L 3G1

Table of Contents

Introduction

The present work provides a selective bibliography of publications on Canadians' social attitudes and beliefs, that appeared from 1972 through 1997.

It is our purpose to provide the beginning researcher with an introduction to some of the scholarly resources available on the topic. This bibliography covers a span of twenty-five years (1972-1997) and includes scholarly books and journal articles. Some doctoral dissertations, master's theses, and government documents have also been included. Newspaper and magazine articles have, for the most part, been excluded. Though our purpose has been to cover the topic as widely as possible and include the works of as many authors as possible, we in no way would like this work to be considered comprehensive.

The contents of the bibliography are divided into ten broad sections. A descriptor index will assist the researcher in locating citations on more precise topics. The information provided in the citations will help the researcher to locate the original resource. To that end we may not always have adhered to the strict rules for bibliographic entry, but we have tried to be consistent. Our intention is to provide the user with as much information about the source as possible and make it easy to locate.

We express our sincere thanks to Dr. Marcella Cristi, who as a graduate student at the University of Waterloo assisted with the research. We are also thankful to Esther Millar, Helena Calogeridis, and Maureen McCormack at the University of Waterloo Library for their editorial work and for seeing this project to its fruition. We also thank the University of Waterloo for the UW Social Sciences and Humanities Research Council grant we received that helped us to begin work on this bibliography.

Shabiran Rahman
Reference/Collections Development Librarian
University of Waterloo Library

Dr. Ronald D. Lambert
Professor
Department of Sociology
University of Waterloo

Section 1

Social Categories and Groups

1. "On the Right Track (National Attitudes of the United Church as Revealed by Observer/Decima Survey)." *The United Church Observer* 52, no. 1 (1988): 36-38.

2. Aboud, Frances E. "Interest in Ethnic Information: A Cross-Cultural Developmental Study." *Canadian Journal of Behavioural Science* 9, no. 2 (1977): 134-46.

3. Aboud, Frances E. "A Test of Ethnocentrism with Young Children." *Canadian Journal of Behavioural Science* 12, no. 3 (1980): 195-209.

4. Abu-Rabia, Salim. "Attitudes and Cultural Background and Their Relationship to English in a Multicultural Social Context: The Case of Male and Female Arab Immigrants in Canada." *Educational Psychology* 15, no. 3 (1995): 323-36.

5. Alberta Premier's Council on the Status of Persons with Disabilities. *Towards a New Vision of Abilities in Alberta*. Edmonton, AB: Premier's Council on the Status of Persons with Disabilities, 1989.

6. Allodi, F., and A. Rojas. "Arauco: The Role of a Housing Cooperative Community in the Mental Health and Social Adaptation of Latin American Refugees in Toronto." *Migration World Magazine* 16, no. 3 (1988): 17-21.

7. Andrews, Donald Arthur et al. *Self-Reported Criminal Propensity and Criminal Behavior: Threats to the Validity of Assessments of Attitudes and Personality*. Ministry of the Solicitor General, Programs Branch User Report, 85-027. Ottawa, ON: Ministry of the Solicitor General, Secretariat, 1985.

8. Angus Reid Group. *Multiculturalism in Canada: Focus Group Summary: Final Report*. Ottawa, ON: Multiculturalism and Citizenship Canada, 1991.

9. Back, J. W. "Transition to Aging and the Self-Image." *Aging and Human Development* 2 (1971): 296-303.

10. Bagley, Christopher, and Loretta Young. "Evaluation of Color and Ethnicity in Young Children in Jamaica, Ghana, England, and Canada." *International Journal of Intercultural Relations* 12, no. 1 (1988): 45-60.

11. Baker, Maureen. *Canadian Youth in a Changing World*. Background Paper for Parliamentarians, 128E. Ottawa, ON: Library of Parliament, Research Branch, 1985.

12. Baker, Peter J. *Student Attitudes toward the Handicapped*. Edmonton, AB: Alberta Education, Planning and Research Branch, 1981.

13. Baltaz, Diane. "Farm Spirituality Gets Only Secondary Concern (Farmers Believe in God, but Have Difficulty Relating to the Church)." *Catholic New Times* 14, no. 6 (1990): 13.

14. Barkely, Jacqueline. "An Examination of the Attitudes and Knowledge Base of Non-Black Social Workers, Counselors and Social Service Workers regarding the Black Community in an Urban Area of Nova Scotia." M.S.W. thesis, Dalhousie University, 1986.

15. Barker, Irwin R., and Raymond F. Currie. "Do Converts Always Make the Most Committed Christians?" *Journal for the Scientific Study of Religion* 24, no. 3 (1985): 305-13.

16. Baron, Stephen W. "The Canadian West Coast Punk Subculture: A Field Study." *Canadian Journal of Sociology* 14, no. 3 (1989): 289-316.

17. Barrett, Stanley R. "White Supremists and Neo-Fascists: Laboratories for the Analysis of Racism in Wider Society." *Canadian Ethnic Studies* 16, no. 1 (1984): 1-15.

18. Bassili, J. N., and J. E. Reil. "On the Dominance of the Old-Age Stereotype." *Journal of Gerontology* 36, no. 6 (1981): 682-88.

19. Bauer, Julien. "Jewish Communities, Jewish Education and Quebec Nationalism." *Social Compass* 31, no. 4 (1984): 391-407.

20. Beattie, John Maurice et al. *Attitudes towards Crime and Punishment in Upper Canada 1830-1850*. Toronto, ON: University of Toronto, Centre of Criminology, 1985.

21. Beland, Francois. "Decision of Elderly Persons to Leave Their Homes." *Gerontologist* 24, no. 2 (1984): 179-85.

22. Berry, John Widdup et al. *Multiculturalism and Ethnic Attitudes in Canada*. Department of the Secretary of State, Multiculturalism Directorate, ss200. Ottawa, ON: Minister of State for Multiculturalism, 1977.

23. Berry, John Widdup, and Rudolf Kalin. "Multicultural and Ethnic Attitudes in Canada: An Overview of the 1991 National Survey." *Canadian Journal of Behavioural Science* 27, no. 3 (1995): 301-20.

24. Bhatia, Kamala. *Report of a Conference on Prejudice and Attitudes in a Multicultural Society*. Hamilton, ON: Mohawk College of Applied Arts and Technology, 1978.

25. Bibby, Reginald Wayne. "Crime and Punishment: A National Reading [Findings of a 1975 Survey on Attitudes Relating to Crime in Canada]." *Social Indicators Research* 9 (March 1981): 1-13.

26. Bibby, Reginald Wayne. "The Delicate Mosaic: A National Examination of Inter-Group Relations in Canada." *Social Indicators Research* 5, no. 2 (1978): 169-79.

27. Bibby, Reginald Wayne. *The Emerging Generation: An Inside Look at Canada's Teenagers*. Toronto, ON: Irwin Publishing, 1985.

28. Bibby, Reginald Wayne. "The Precarious Mosaic: Divergence and Convergence in the Canadian 80s [Public Attitudes toward the Government's Bilingualism Policies and toward Ethnic Minorities]." *Social Indicators Research* 12 (Fall 1983): 169-81.

29. Boldt, Menno. "Normative Evaluations of Suicide and Death: A Cross-Generational Study." *Omega: Journal of Death and Dying* 13, no. 2 (1982-83): 145-57.

30. Bond, John B. "Familial Support of the Elderly in a Rural Mennonite Community." *Canadian Journal on Aging* 6, no. 1 (1987): 7-17.

31. Boyer, Eunice Felter. "Review Essay: Ethnicity and Aging." *Journal of Cross Cultural Gerontology* 2, no. 1 (1987): 107-13.

32. Brauner, Sheila S. "Impact of the Confused Elderly on the Lucid Aged in a Nursing Home." *Journal of Gerontological Social Work* 14, no. 1-2 (1989): 137-52.

33. Breton, Raymond Jules. *The Ethnic Community as a Resource in Relation to Group Problems: Perceptions and Attitudes*. Ethnic Pluralism Paper, no. 2. Toronto, ON: University of Toronto, Centre for Urban and Community Studies, 1981.

34. Brillon, Yves et al. "Attitudes of the Canadian Public toward Crime Policies/Review." *Canadian Journal of Criminology* 28, no. 1 (1986): 87-89.

35. Brillon, Yves. *Victimization and Fear of Crime among the Elderly.* Toronto, ON: Butterworths, 1987.

36. Brinkerhoff, Merlin B., and Marlene MacKie. "Religion and Gender: A Comparison of Canadian and American Student Attitudes." *Journal of Marriage and the Family* 47, no. 2 (1985): 415-29.

37. Brinkerhoff, Merlin B., and Marlene MacKie. "Religious Denominations' Impact upon Gender Attitudes: Some Methodological Implications." *Review of Religious Research* 25, no. 4 (1984): 365-78.

38. Burke, Mary Anne. "Implications of an Aging Society." *Canadian Social Trends* 20 (Spring 1991): 6-8.

39. Canada. Department of Multiculturalism and Citizenship Canada. *Eliminating Racial Discrimination in Canada.* Ottawa, ON: The Department, 1989.

40. Canada. Ministry of State for Multiculturalism, and Berry, John Widdup. *Summary, Multiculturalism and Ethnic Attitudes in Canada.* N.p., 1976.

41. Canada. Ministry of the Solicitor General. Programs Branch. *Fear of Crime, Victimization and Attitudes to Protective Measures.* Programs Branch User Report, 84-061. Ottawa, ON: Ministry of the Solicitor General, 1984.

42. Canadian Human Rights Commission. *Discrimination in Canada - A Survey of Knowledge, Attitudes and Practices Concerned with Discrimination.* Ottawa, ON: The Commission, 1979.

43. Canadian Rehabilitation Council for the Disabled. *Inventory of Materials for Use in Reducing Attitudinal Barriers towards Disabled Persons.* Ottawa, ON: Transport Canada, Policy and Coordination, 1988.

44. Carson, W. McMullin. "A Canadian Therapeutic Community for Disruptive Youths." *International Journal of Offender Therapy and Comparative Criminology* 17, no. 3 (1973): 268-84.

45. Cartwright, Barry Edward. "Prisoner Attitudes toward Crime, Politics, and the Socioeconomic System: The Politicized Prisoner Phenomenon." Master's thesis, University of British Columbia, 1983.

46. Catton, Katherine. *Adolescent Beliefs and Practices regarding the Law of Minors' Medical Consent: A Pilot Study*. Child in the City Report, no. 7. Toronto, ON: University of Toronto, Centre for Urban and Community Studies, 1980.

47. Chandra, Kananur V. *The Adjustment and Attitudes of East Indian Students in Canada*. Fort Valley, GA: R. D. Reed, 1974.

48. Chappell, Nenna L., and M. J. Penning. "Trend Away from Institutionalization: Humanism or Economic Efficiency?" *Research on Aging* 1, no. 3 (1979): 361-87.

49. Cheal, David. "Religion and the Social Order." *Canadian Journal of Sociology* 3, no. 1 (1978): 61-69.

50. Chellam, G. "Intergenerational Affinities: Symmetrical Life Experiences of the Young Adults and the Aging in Canadian Society." *International Journal of Aging and Human Development* 12, no. 2 (1981): 79-92.

51. Clairmont, D. H., and F. C. Wien. "Race Relations in Canada." *Sociological Focus* 9, no. 2 (1976): 185-97.

52. Cohn, Werner. "English and French Canadian Public Opinion on Jews and Israel: Some Poll Data." *Canadian Ethnic Studies* 11, no. 2 (1979): 31-48.

53. Connidis, Ingrid. "The Subjective Experience of Aging: Correlates of Divergent Views." *Canadian Journal on Aging* 8, no. 1 (1989): 7-18.

54. Cook, Philip. "Chronic Illness Beliefs and the Role of Social Networks among Chinese, Indian, and Angloceltic Canadians." *Journal of Cross-Cultural Psychology* 25, no. 4 (1994): 452-65.

55. Courtis, M. C., and L. Dussuyer. *Attitudes to Crime and the Police in Toronto: A Report on Some Survey Findings*. Research Report, 1. Toronto, ON: University of Toronto, Centre of Criminology, 1970.

56. Creechan, James H. *Attitudes toward Crime and Law Enforcement: A Comparison of Canadian and American Data*. Edmonton Area Series, 04. Edmonton, AB: University of Alberta, Department of Sociology, 1978.

57. Crysdale, Stewart. *The Changing Church in Canada; Beliefs and Social Attitudes of United Church People*. Toronto, ON: United Church of Canada, Board of Evangelism and Social Service, Evangelism Resource Committee, 1965.

58. Crysdale, Stewart. "Some Problematic Aspects of Religion in Canada." *Sociological Focus* 9, no. 2 (1976): 137-48.

59. Curtis, James E., and Ronald D. Lambert. "Status Dissatisfaction and Out-Group Rejection: Cross-Cultural Comparisons within Canada." *Canadian Review of Sociology and Anthropology* 12, no. 2 (1975): 178-92.

60. Daciuk, Joanne F., and Victor W. Marshall. "Health Concerns as a Deterrent to Seasonal Migration of Elderly Canadians." *Social Indicators Research* 22, no. 2 (1990): 181-97.

61. Dargyay, Lobsang. "Tibetans in Alberta and Their Cultural Identity." *Canadian Ethnic Studies* 20, no. 2 (1988): 114-23.

62. Devine, B. A. "Attitudes of the Elderly toward Religion." *Journal of Gerontological Nursing* 6, no. 11 (1980): 679-87.

63. Doob, Anthony N. *Crime: Some Views of the Canadian Public*. Toronto, ON: University of Toronto, Centre of Criminology, 1982.

64. Dooley, Stephen, and Gail B. Frankel. "Improving Attitudes toward Elderly People: Evaluation of an Intervention Program for Adolescents." *Canadian Journal of Aging* 9, no. 4 (1990): 400-409.

65. Douglas, K. *Spousal Support under the Divorce Act: A New Direction*. Rev. ed. Ottawa, ON: Library of Parliament, Research Branch, 1993.

66. Downe-Wamboldt, Barbara L., and Patricia M. Melanson. "Attitudes of Baccalaureate Student Nurses toward Aging and the Aged: Results of a Longitudinal Study." *Educational Gerontology* 16, no. 1 (1990): 49-59.

67. Driedger, Leo. "Alert Opening and Closing: Mennonite Rural-Urban Changes." *Rural Sociology* 60 (Summer 1995): 323-32.

68. Driedger, Leo et al. "Dualistic and Wholistic Views of God and the World: Consequences for Social Action." *Review of Religious Research* 24, no. 3 (1983): 225-44.

69. Filson, Glen. "Class and Ethnic Differences in Canadians' Attitudes to Native People's Rights and Immigration." *Canadian Review of Sociology and Anthropology* 20, no. 4 (1983): 454-82.

70. Flynn, Brian J. "A Study of Religious Beliefs and Moral Commitments of Roman Catholics: Implications for Religious Socialization." Ph.D. diss., University of Calgary, 1981.

71. Forgay, Beryl A. (Beryl Alice). "Attitudes in Saskatchewan Society toward People Labelled Mentally Retarded." Master's thesis, University of Regina, 1986.

72. Frideres, James S. "British Canadian Attitudes toward Minority Ethnic Groups in Canada." *Ethnicity* 5, no. 1 (1978): 20-32.

73. Frideres, James S. "The Death of Hutterite Culture." *Phylon* 33, no. 3 (1972): 260-65.

74. Fry, P. S. "Factor Analytic Investigation of Home-Bound Elderly Individuals' Concerns about Death and Dying, and Their Coping Responses." *Journal of Clinical Psychology* 46, no. 6 (1990): 737-48.

75. Gardner, Robert. *Ethnic Stereotypes: The Implications of Measurement Strategy*. Research Bulletin, no. 642. London, ON: University of Western Ontario, Department of Psychology, 1986.

76. Gee, Ellen M., and Jean E. Veevers. "Religiously Unaffiliated Canadians: Sex, Age, and Regional Variations." *Social Indicators Research* 21, no. 6 (1989): 611-27.

77. Goldberg, Gerald Elliot. *Attitudes, Communication and Occupational Safety: Overcoming Attitudes toward Disabled Employees*. Toronto, ON: Ontario Ministry of Labour, Occupational Health and Safety Division, Special Studies and Services Branch, Safety Studies Service, 1982.

78. Goldfarb Consultants Limited. *National Attitudes towards Crime and Gun Control*. Ottawa, ON: Ministry of Supply and Services Canada, 1977.

79. Grabb, Edward G. "Sense of Control over Life Circumstances: Changing Patterns for French and English Canadians." *Canadian Review of Sociology and Anthropology* 19, no. 3 (1982): 360-76.

80. Grabb, Edward G., and Ronald D. Lambert. "The Subjective Meanings of Social Class among Canadians." *Canadian Journal of Sociology* 7, no. 3 (1982): 297-307.

81. Graham, Ian D., and Paul M. Baker. "Status, Age and Gender: Perceptions of Old and Young People." *Canadian Journal of Aging* 8, no. 3 (1989): 255-67.

82. Griffin, Ronald J. "Social Change, Belief and Pentecostalism in the Roman Catholic Church." Master's thesis, York University, 1976.

83. Guinan, W., and Ontario. Ministry of Community and Social Services. Long-Term Study of Aging. *Attitudes toward Retirement Found in a Longitudinal Study of Aging.* Toronto, ON: Ontario Ministry of Community and Social Services, Office on Aging Branch, 1972.

84. Guppy, Neil. "Magic of 65: Issues and Evidence in the Mandatory Retirement Debate." *Canadian Journal on Aging* 8, no. 2 (1989): 173-86.

85. Gupta, Dipankar. "Racism without Colour: The Catholic Ethnic and Ethnicity in Quebec." *Race and Class* 25, no. 1 (1983): 23-44.

86. Gutman, Gloria M., and Stephen L. Mulstein. *Attitudes of Seniors to Special Retirement Housing, Life Tenancy Arrangements and Other Housing Options.* Ottawa, ON: Canada Mortgage and Housing Corporation, Research Division, 1987.

87. Hagan, John et al. "Explaining Official Deliquency: A Spatial Study of Class, Conflict and Control." *Sociological Quarterly* 19, no. 3 (1978): 386-98.

88. Harney, Robert F. "Men without Women: Italian Migrants in Canada, 1885-1930." *Canadian Ethnic Studies* 11, no. 1 (1979): 29-47.

89. Harrell, W. Andrew. "Masculinity and Farming Related Accidents." *Sex Roles* 15, no. 9-10 (1986): 467-78.

90. Hartnagel, Timothy F. "Perception and Fear of Crime: Implications for Neighborhood Cohesion, Social Activity, and Community Affect." *Social Forces* 57, no. 1 (1979): 176-93.

91. Hartnagel, Timothy F., and Leo Klug. "Changing Religious Attitudes and Participation among Catholics in the Post Vatican II Church: Some Canadian Data." *Sociological Analysis* 51 (Winter 1990): 347-61.

92. Hartse, Caroline. "Social and Religious Change among Contemporary Hutterites." *Folk* 36 (1995): 109-30.

93. Hetherington, Robert W. "Evaluation of a Regional Resource Center for Multiply-Handicapped Retarded Children." *International Journal of Rehabilitation Research* 4, no. 1 (1981): 73-75.

94. Hill, Michael, and Wiebe Zwaga. "The "Nones" Story: A Comparative Analysis of Religious Nonalignment." *New Zealand Sociology* 4, no. 2 (1989): 164-89.

95. Hobart, Charles W. "Sources of Egalitarianism in Young Unmarried Canadians." *Canadian Journal of Sociology* 6, no. 3 (1981): 261-82.

96. Hunsberger, Bruce. "Racial Awareness and Preference of White and Indian Canadian Children." *Canadian Journal of Behavioural Science* 10, no. 2 (1978): 176-80.

97. Hunsberger, Bruce. "Religion, Age, Life Satisfaction, and Perceived Sources of Religiousness: A Study of Older Persons." *Journal of Gerontology* 40, no. 5 (1985): 615-20.

98. Hunsberger, Bruce, and Jeff Ennis. "Experimenter Effects in Studies of Religious Attitudes." *Journal for the Scientific Study of Religion* 21, no. 2 (1982): 131-37.

99. Hylton, John H. et al. *Public Attitudes about Crime and the Police in Regina*. Regina, SK: Regina Police Department, 1979.

100. Jamal, Muhammed, and Jamal A. Badawi. "Nonstandard Work Schedules and Work and Nonwork Experiences of Muslim Immigrants: A Study of a Minority in the Majority." *Journal of Social Behavior and Personality* 10, no. 2 (1995): 395-408.

101. Kalin, Rudolf. "Ethnic and Multicultural Attitudes among Children in a Canadian City." *Canadian Ethnic Studies* 11, no. 1 (1979): 69-81.

102. Kanagy, Conrad, and Leo Driedger. "Changing Mennonite Values: Attitudes on Women, Politics, and Peace 1972-1989." *Review of Religious Research* 37, no. 4 (1996): 342-53.

103. Kapos, A., and D. Smith. *Identifying Standard Attitudes toward Senescence (Aging)*. Toronto, ON: Ontario Homes for the Aged - Office on Aging Branch; Ontario Welfare Council, Section on Aging, 1972.

104. Keddie, Vincent Gordon. "A Study of Manual Workers' Attitudes toward Social Class in Four Ontario Communities." Ph.D. diss., McMaster University, 1974.

105. Keddy, Barbara, and Dianne Young. "Meaning of Holidays in a Nursing Home." *Geriatric Nursing* 5, no. 1 (1984): 43-46.

106. Kehoe, John W. et al. "Changing Negative Attitudes toward Japanese and East Indian Canadians in Elementary School Children by Using Classical Conditioning Procedures." *Alberta Journal of Educational Research* 24, no. 4 (1978): 257-61.

107. Kendis, Randall Jay. *Attitude of Gratitude: The Adaptation to Aging of the Elderly Japanese in America.* Immigrant Communities and Ethnic Minorities in the United States and Canada, no. 33. New York, NY: AMS Press, 1989.

108. Kimmel, D. C. et al. "Retirement Choice and Retirement Satisfaction." *Journal of Gerontology* 33, no. 4 (1978): 575-85.

109. Klein, John F. et al. "Experience with the Police and Attitude towards the Police." *Canadian Journal of Sociology* 3, no. 4 (1978): 441-56.

110. Knox, V. J., and W. L. Gekoski. "Effect of Judgment Context on Assessments of Age Groups." *Canadian Journal of Aging* 8, no. 3 (1989): 244-54.

111. Koenig, Daniel J. "Police Perceptions of Public Respect and Extra-Legal Use of Force: A Reconsideration of Folk Wisdom and Pluralistic Ignorance." *Canadian Journal of Sociology* 1, no. 3 (1975): 313-24.

112. Kostash, Myrna. *Long Way from Home: The Story of the Sixties Generation in Canada.* Toronto, ON: J. Lorimer, 1980.

113. Kurian, George. "Social and Financial Provisions for the Elderly in Canada -- a Case-Study in the City of Calgary." *Indian Journal of Social Research* 13, no. 2 (1972): 119-26.

114. Kwan, Yui-Huen. "Attitudes of Social Work Students toward Older Persons." M.S.W. thesis, University of British Columbia, 1982.

115. Labun, Evelyn. "Vietnamese Woman in Canada: Learning about a Different Perspective on Health." *The Canadian Nurse* 84, no. 8 (1988): 49-50.

116. Lambert, Ronald D. et al. "Canadians' Beliefs about Differences between Social Classes." *Canadian Journal of Sociology* 11, no. 4 (1986): 379-99.

117. Lambert, Ronald D., and James E. Curtis. "Opposition to Multiculturalism among Quebecois and English-Canadians." *Canadian Review of Sociology and Anthropology* 20, no. 2 (1983): 193-207.

118. Lambert, Wallace E. et al. "Greek Canadians' Attitudes toward Own Group and Other Canadian Ethnic Groups: A Test of the Multiculturalism Hypothesis." *Canadian Journal of Behavioural Science* 18, no. 1 (1986): 35-51.

119. Lamy, Paul. "Language and Ethnicity: A Study of Bilingualism, Ethnic Identity and Ethnic Attitudes." Ph.D. diss., McMaster University, 1976.

120. Lanca, Margaret et al. "Effects of Language Choice on Acculturation: A Study of Portuguese Immigrants in a Multicultural Setting." *Journal of Language and Social Psychology* 13, no. 3 (1994): 315-30.

121. Lasry, Jean Claude. "Sephardim and Ashkenazim in Montreal." *Contemporary Jewry* 6, no. 2 (1983): 26-33.

122. Lee, John Alan. "Invisible Men: Canada's Aging Homosexuals. Can They Be Assimilated into Canada's 'Liberated' Gay Communities?" *Canadian Journal on Aging* 8, no. 1 (1989): 79-97.

123. Lester, David et al. "Job Satisfaction, Cynicism and Belief in an External Locus of Control: A Study of Police in Four Nations." *Police Studies* 5, no. 2 (1982): 6-9.

124. Leung, Hok Lin. "Housing Concerns of Elderly Homeowners." *Journal of Aging Studies* 1, no. 4 (1987): 379-91.

125. Levi, Michael. *Regulating Fraud: White-Collar Crime and the Criminal Process.* London, ON: Tavistock Publications, 1987.

126. Levine, Saul V., and Nancy E. Salter. "Youth and Contemporary Religious Movements: Psychosocial Findings." *Canadian Psychiatric Association Journal* 21, no. 6 (1976): 411-20.

127. Li, Peter S. "Prejudice against Asians in a Canadian City." *Canadian Ethnic Studies* 11, no. 2 (1979): 70-77.

128. Loomis, Rhonda A., and Cheryl D. Thomas. "Elderly Women in Nursing Home and Independent Residence: Health, Body Attitudes, Self-Esteem and Life Satisfaction." *Canadian Journal on Aging* 10, no. 3 (1991): 224-31.

129. Lupul, Manoly R. "Networking, Discrimination and Multiculturalism as a Social Philosophy." *Canadian Ethnic Studies* 21, no. 2 (1989): 1-12.

130. Mackie, Marlene, and Merlin B. Brinkerhoff. "Ethnic Identification: Both Sides of the Border." *Canadian Ethnic Studies* 20, no. 2 (1989): 101-13.

131. Mackie, Marlene, and Merlin B. Brinkerhoff. "Ethnicity's Impact upon Familial/Gender Attitudes and Behaviors: Social Reality or Social Fiction?" *Canadian Ethnic Studies* 14, no. 2 (1982): 99-113.

132. MacLean, Michael J., and Sheila M. Chown. "Just World Beliefs and Attitudes toward Helping Elderly People: A Comparison of British and Canadian University Students." *International Journal of Aging and Human Development* 26, no. 4 (1988): 249-60.

133. Madden, Patrick G., and Leah R. Lambert. *Length of Time in Vanier, Attitudes and First Year Recidivism*. Vanier Centre for Women Research Report, 2. Toronto, ON: Ontario Ministry of Correctional Services, 1974.

134. Manthe, Rene. "When Police Shoot Indians: Manitoba Promises an Inquiry, but it's Unlikely to Stem Anger." *Alberta (Western) Report* 15, no. 15 (1988): 35.

135. Mantte, J. "Nursing Care of the Aged in Canada." *Journal of Gerontological Nursing* 7, no. 11 (1981): 671-76.

136. Markus, Roberta L., and Donald V. Schwarz. "Soviet Jewish Emigres in Toronto: Ethnic Self-Identity and Issues of Integration." *Canadian Ethnic Studies* 16, no. 2 (1984): 71-88.

137. Matthews, Anne Martin, and Kathleen H. Brown. "Retirement as a Critical Life Event: The Differential Experiences of Women and Men." *Research on Aging* 9, no. 4 (1987): 548-71.

138. Mercer, G. et al. "Adolescent Drug Use and Attitudes toward the Family." *Canadian Journal of Behavioural Science* 10, no. 1 (1978): 79-90.

139. Milner, Joanne. "National Access Awareness Week." *Rehabilitation Digest* 20, no. 1 (1989): 10-11.

140. Moghaddam, Fathali et al. "Integration Strategies and Attitudes toward the Built Environment: A Study of Haitian and Indian Immigrant Women in Montreal." *Canadian Journal of Behavioural Science* 21, no. 2 (1989): 160-73.

141. Moody, Barry M. *Repent and Believe: The Baptist Experience in Maritime Canada*. Hantsport, NS: Lancelot Press for Acadia Divinity College and Baptist Historical Committee of the United Baptist Convention of the Atlantic Provinces, 1980.

142. Morrison, Suzanne. "Handicapped in the Workplace: Physically Handicapped Employees Feel Their Needs and Human Rights Are Far from Being Respected As They Encounter Hiring and Attitude Problems among Employers [Canada]." *Metropolitan Toronto Board of Trade Journal* 69 (January 1979): 21-28.

143. Mossey, J. M. et al. "Manitoba Longitudinal Study on Aging: Description and Methods." *Gerontologist* 21, no. 5 (1981): 551-58.

144. Mulawka, Edward J., and Canada. Employment and Immigration Commission. *Immigrants to Newfoundland: Their Settlement Experiences and Attitudes*. St. John's, NF: Employment and Immigration Canada, 1983.

145. Myles, J. F. "Institutionalization and Sick Role Identification among the Elderly." *American Sociological Review* 43, no. 4 (1978): 508-21.

146. Naidoo, Josephine C., and J. Campbell Davis. "Canadian South Asian Women in Transition: A Dualistic View of Life." *Journal of Comparative Family Studies* 19, no. 2 (1988): 311-27.

147. National Task Force on Suicide in Canada. *Suicide in Canada / Report of the National Task Force on Suicide in Canada*. Ottawa, ON: Health and Welfare Canada, 1987.

148. Naus, Peter J., and John P. Theis. "The Significance of Fatherly Affirmation for a Man's Psychological Well-Being: A Comparison of Canadian and Dutch University Students." *Canadian Journal of Human Sexuality* 4, no. 4 (1995): 237-45.

149. Noble, Cinnie. "Sensitivity-Awareness Training: Removing Attitudinal Barriers." *Rehabilitation Digest* 20, no. 1 (1989): 6-7.

150. Olsen, I. A. "Attitudes of Nursing Students toward Aging and the Aged." *Gerontology and Geriatrics Education* 2, no. 3 (1982): 233-36.

151. Ontario Advisory Council for Disabled Persons. *Workable: Fulfilling the Potential of People with Disabilities*. Toronto, ON: The Council, 1990.

152. Ontario Advisory Council on Senior Citizens. *Aging Together - An Exploration of Attitudes towards Aging in Multicultural Ontario.* Toronto, ON: The Council, 1989.

153. Ontario. Ministry of Tourism and Recreation. Recreation Branch. *Retirement Planning for Small Communities in Ontario.* Toronto, ON: Ontario Ministry of Tourism and Recreation, 1987.

154. Pak, Anita Wan Ping et al. "Social-Psychological Correlates of Experienced Discrimination: Test of the Double Jeopardy Hypothesis." *International Journal of Intercultural Relations* 15, no. 2 (1991): 243-54.

155. Palmer, Douglas L. et al. "A Factor-Analytic Study of English and French Forms of a Measure of Attitudes toward Convicts and Ex-Convicts." *Canadian Journal of Criminology* 31 (April 1989): 155-67.

156. Pastalan, Leon A. "The Retirement Community Movement: Contemporary Issues." *Journal of Housing for the Elderly* 5, no. 2 (1989): 5-81.

157. Peitchinis, Stephen G. "The Attitude of Trade Unions towards Technological Changes [Emphasis on Canada]." *Industrial Relations* 38, no. 1 (1983): 104-18.

158. Perrin, Robin D. "American Religion in the Post-Aquarian Age: Values and Demographic Factors in Church Growth and Decline." *Journal for the Scientific Study of Religion* 28, no. 1 (1989): 75- 89.

159. Piepkorn, Arthur Carl. *Profiles in Belief: The Religious Bodies of the United States and Canada.* New York: Harper & Row, 1977-1979.

160. Poetschke, Donna Marie. "Social Class and Attitudes in Alberta, 1971." Master's thesis, University of Alberta, 1976.

161. Price, K. F. et al. "Retirement Timing and Retirement Satisfaction." *Aging and Work* 2, no. 4 (1979): 235-45.

162. Ramsay, Richard, and Christopher Bagley. "The Prevalence of Suicidal Behaviors, Attitudes and Associated Social Experiences in an Urban Population." *Suicide and Life Threatening Behaviour* 15, no. 3 (1985): 151-67.

163. Redekop, Calvin. "The Social Ecology of Communal Socialization." *International Review of Modern Sociology* 6, no. 1 (1976): 113-25.

164. Reitz, Jeffrey G., and Raymond Jules Breton. *The Illusion of Difference: Realities of Ethnicity in Canada and the United States.* Observations, 37. Toronto, ON: C. D. Howe Institute, 1994.

165. Rinehart, James W., and Ishmael O. Okraku. "A Study of Class Consciousness." *Canadian Review of Sociology and Anthropology* 11, no. 3 (1974): 197-213.

166. Rissanen, Pekka. *Multicultural Awareness on Prince Edward Island: An Inquiry into Attitudes toward Immigration: Ethnic Personality and Multiculturalism.* Monographs on Multiculturalism, no. 3. Charlottetown, PE: Prince Edward Island Multicultural Council, 1981.

167. Roadburg, A. "Perceptions of Work and Leisure among the Elderly." *Gerontologist* 21, no. 2 (1981): 142-45.

168. Robinson, Robert R. "Older Can Be Happier (Research by Dr. Alex Michalos of the University of Guelph)." *Discovery* 9, no. 7 (1988): 12-13.

169. Rostum, Hussein. *Attitudes of Canadians towards Persons with Disabilities.* Ottawa, ON: TEEGA Research Consultants, 1988.

170. Rotenberg, Ken J. "Measure of the Trust Beliefs of Elderly Individuals." *International Journal of Aging and Human Development* 30, no. 2 (1990): 141-52.

171. Russell, Peter A. *Attitudes to Social Structure and Mobility in Upper Canada, 1815-1840: "Here We Are Laird Ourselves."* Canadian Studies, vol. 6. Lewiston, NY: E. Mellen Press, 1990.

172. Sacco, Vincent F. "City Size and Perceptions of Crime." *Canadian Journal of Sociology* 10, no. 3 (1985): 277-93.

173. Sacco, Vincent F. *Special Research Report: Factors Associated with Public Perceptions of Crime.* Burnaby, BC: Simon Fraser University, Criminology Research Centre, 1984.

174. Sachdev, Itesh et al. "Language Attitudes and Vitality Perceptions: Intergenerational Effects amongst Chinese Canadian Communities." *Journal of Language and Social Psychology* 6, no. 3-4 (1987): 287-307.

175. Sarna, Jonathan D. "Jewish Immigration to North America: The Canadian Experience (1870- 1900)." *Jewish Journal of Sociology* 18, no. 1 (1976): 31-41.

176. Schissel, Bernard et al. "Social and Economic Context and Attitudes toward Immigrants in Canadian Cities." *International Migration Review* 23 (Summer 1989): 289-308.

177. Schneiderman, Eta. "Sex Differences in the Development of Children's Ethnic and Language Attitudes." *International Journal of the Sociology of Language* 38 (1982): 31-44.

178. Schoenfeld, Stuart. "The Jewish Religion in North America: Canadian and American Comparisons." *Canadian Journal of Sociology* 3, no. 2 (1978): 209-31.

179. Searle, Mark S. *Leisure and Aging in Manitoba: Executive Summary - A Report to Manitoba Culture Heritage and Recreation*. Winnipeg, MB: Manitoba Culture, Heritage and Recreation, 1987.

180. Shapiro, E., and N. P. Roos. "Retired and Employed Elderly Persons: Their Utilization of Health Care Services." *Gerontologist* 22, no. 2 (1982): 187-93.

181. Smith, Dorothy E. "Racism - What is Our Responsibility?" *Society* 2, no. 1 (1978): 4.

182. Stephens, M., and Alberta. Department of Social Services and Community Health. Senior Citizens Bureau. *Attitudes towards Aging, Old Age and Older Persons - A Review and Discussion*. Profile Index Canadian Provincial Publications, 78-0888. Edmonton, AB: Alberta Department of Social Services and Community Health, Senior Citizens Bureau, 1978.

183. Stewart, Garth A. "The Relationship between Adolescents' Concern over the Threat of Nuclear War and Several Personality Dimensions." *Canadian Journal of Behavioural Science* 20, no. 4 (1988): 452-60.

184. Stone, Daniel. "Winnipeg's Polish Language Newspapers and Their Attitudes towards Jews and Ukrainians between the Two World Wars." *Canadian Ethnic Studies* 21, no. 2 (1989): 26-37.

185. Storm, Christine. "Obligations for Care: Beliefs in a Small Canadian Town." *Canadian Journal of Aging* 4, no. 2 (1985): 75-85.

186. Strange, Heather et al. *Aging and Cultural Diversity: New Directions and Annotated Bibliography*. South Hadley, MA: Bergin and Garvey Publishers, 1987.

187. Stroud, Carsten. *The Blue Wall: The Street Cops in Canada*. Toronto, ON: McClelland and Stewart, 1984.

188. Sugeman, Pamela, and H. K. Nishio. "Socialization and Cultural Duality among Aging Japanese Canadians." *Canadian Ethnic Studies* 15, no. 3 (1983): 17-35.

189. Sulerzhitsky, L. A. *To America with the Doukhobors*. Canadian Plains Studies, 12. Regina, SK: Canadian Plains Research Center, 1982.

190. Synge, Jane. "Avoided Conversations: How Parents and Children Delay Talking about Widowhood and Dependency in Later Life." *Aging and Society* 8, no. 3 (1988): 321-25.

191. Tanner, Julian, and Rhonda Cockerill. "In Search of Working-Class Ideology: A Test of Two Perspectives." *Sociological Quarterly* 27, no. 3 (1986): 389-402.

192. Tarasoff, Koozma J. "The Coming of Age of the Doukhobors in the 1980s." *Canadian Ethnic Studies* 19, no. 2 (1987): 124-30.

193. Taylor, Donald M. et al. "Cultural Insecurity and Attitudes toward Multiculturalism and Ethnic Groups in Canada." *Canadian Ethnic Studies* 11, no. 2 (1979): 19-30.

194. Taylor, Donald M. et al. "Perceptions of Cultural Differences and Language Use: A Field Study in a Bilingual Environment." *Canadian Journal of Behavioural Science* 10, no. 3 (1978): 181- 91.

195. Tebeje, A. *Cultural Interaction of Canadians and Ethiopian Newcomers in Canada*. Ottawa, ON: Employment and Immigration Canada, 1989.

196. Thorns, David C. "The Production of Homelessness: From Individual Failure to System Inadequacies." *Housing Studies* 4, no. 4 (1989): 253-66.

197. Thornton, James E., and John B. Collins. "Patterns of Leisure and Physical Activities among Older Adults." *Activities, Adaptation and Aging* 8, no. 2 (1986): 5-27.

198. Thornton, James E., and Earl R. Winkler. *Ethnics and Aging: The Right to Live, the Right to Die*. Vancouver, BC: University of British Columbia Press, 1988.

199. Thornton, Leonard M. "People and the Police: An Analysis of Factors Associated with Police Evaluation and Support." *Canadian Journal of Sociology* 1, no. 3 (1975): 325-42.

200. Tienhaara, Nancy. *Canadian Views on Immigration and Population: An Analysis of Post-War Gallup Polls.* Ottawa, ON: Manpower and Immigration, 1974.

201. Toronto. Ontario Office for Disabled Persons. *The Needs and Attitudes of Disabled Ontarians.* Toronto, ON: Environics Research Group, 1989.

202. Tunteng, P. Kiven. "Racism and the Montreal Computer Incident of 1969." *Race* 14, no. 3 (1973): 229-40.

203. Ungerleider, Charles S. "Intercultural Awareness and Sensitivity of Canadian Police Officers." *Canadian Public Administration* 32, no. 4 (1989): 612-22.

204. Ungerleider, Charles S. "Police Intercultural Education: Promoting Understanding and Empathy between Police and Ethnic Communities." *Canadian Ethnic Studies* 17, no. 1 (1985): 51-66.

205. Vinish, Mary T. *Modification of Children's Attitudes toward the Handicapped: An Assessment of the Effectiveness of a Specific Unit of Study.* Research Centre Report, no. 19. Regina, SK: Saskatchewan School Trustees' Association, 1974.

206. Walker, J. W. et al. "Retirement Style and Retirement Satisfaction: Retirees Aren't All Alike." *International Journal of Aging and Human Development* 12, no. 4 (1980-81): 267-81.

207. Wanner, Richad A., and T. C. Caputo. "Punitiveness, Fear of Crime, and Perceptions of Violence." *Canadian Journal of Sociology* 12, no. 4 (1987): 331-44.

208. Ward, W. Peter. *White Canada Forever: Popular Attitudes and Public Policy toward Orientals in British Columbia.* Montreal, PQ: McGill-Queen's University Press, 1978.

209. Weinfeld, Morton. "The Jews of Quebec: Perceived Antisemitism, Segregation, and Emigration." *Jewish Journal of Sociology* 22, no. 1 (1980): 5-20.

210. Weinfeld, Morton et al. "Long Term Effects of the Holocaust on Selected Social Attitudes and Behaviour of Survivors: A Cautionary Note." *Social Forces* 60, no. 1 (1981): 1-19.

211. Weinfeld, Morton. "Myth and Reality in the Canadian Mosaic: 'Affective Ethnicity'." *Canadian Ethnic Studies* 13, no. 3 (1981): 80-100.

212. White, James, and James S. Frideres. "Race Prejudice and Racism: A Distinction." *Canadian Review of Sociology and Anthropology* 14, no. 1 (1977): 81-90.

213. White, Philip G. *English-Canadians and French-Canadians Attitudes toward Outgroups: Findings and Interpretations from National Surveys.* N.p., 1987.

214. Wister, Andrew V., and Thomas K. Burch. "Attitudes of the Elderly towards Living Arrangements: Conceptual and Methodological Issues." *Journal of Housing for the Elderly* 5, no. 2 (1989): 5-18.

215. Woon, Yuen-Fong. "Social Discontinuities in North American Chinese Communities: The Case of the Kwaan in Vancouver and Victoria, 1880-1960." *Canadian Review of Sociology and Anthropology* 15, no. 4 (1978): 443-51.

216. Wormith, J. S. "Attitude and Behavior Change of Correctional Clientele: A Three Year Follow-Up." *Criminology* 22, no. 4 (1984): 595-618.

217. Wormith, J. S. et al. "Characteristics of Protective Custody Offenders in a Provincial Correction Centre." *Canadian Journal of Criminology* 30, no. 1 (1988): 39-58.

218. Zamble, Edward, and Phyllis Annesley. "Some Determinants of Public Attitudes toward the Police." *Journal of Police Science and Administration* 15 (December 1987): 285-90.

219. Zeman, Jarold K., and Walter Klaassen. *The Believers' Church in Canada: Addresses and Papers from the Study Conference in Winnipeg, May 15-18, 1978.* Brantford, ON: Baptist Federation of Canada; Winnipeg, MB: Mennonite Central Committee, 1979.

220. Ziegler, Suzanne. "Measuring Inter-Ethnic Attitudes in a Multi-Ethnic Context." *Canadian Ethnic Studies* 12, no. 3 (1980): 45-55.

221. Zussman, David. "The Image of the Public Service in Canada [Comparison with Attitudes toward the Private Sector]." *Canadian Public Administration* 25 (Spring 1982): 63-80.

Section 2

Social Institutions

222. Adair, John G., and Robert Davidson. *Research Activity in the Social Sciences: A Review of Funding, Productivity, and Attitudes of University-Based Social Sciences.* Ottawa, ON: Social Sciences and Humanities Research Council of Canada, 1984.

223. Adrien, Alix A. et al. "Knowledge, Attitudes, Beliefs and Practices Related to AIDS among Montreal Residents of Haitian Origin." *Canadian Journal of Public Health* 81, no. 2 (1990): 129-34.

224. Alberta. Department of Health and Social Development. *Public Attitudes toward Public Assistance in Alberta, April 25, 1973.* Edmonton, AB: The Department, 1973.

225. Aleong, Stanley. "The Role of the Technical School in the Knowledge and Use of Prescribed Automotive Terminology among Students in Quebec, Canada." *International Journal of the Sociology of Language* 38 (1982): 45-70.

226. Allard, Real, and Rodrigue Landry. "Subjective Ethnolinguistic Vitality: A Comparison of Two Measures." *International Journal of the Sociology of Language* 108 (1994): 117-44.

227. Andrews, Donald Arthur, and J. S. Wormith. *Criminal Sentiments and Criminal Behaviour.* User Report, no. 1984-30. Ottawa, ON: Solicitor General Canada, Programs Branch, 1984.

228. Andrews, Margaret W. "Medical Services in Vancouver, 1886-1920: A Study in the Interplay of Attitudes, Medical Knowledge, and Administrative Structures." Ph.D. diss., University of British Columbia, 1979.

229. Appleby, Lon. "Working with AIDS (Attitude of Businesses towards Employees with AIDS)." *Metropolitan Toronto Business Journal* 80, no. 10 (1990): 22-25.

230. Armstrong-Esther, Chris, and W. E. Hewitt. "AIDS: The Knowledge and Attitudes of Nurses." *The Canadian Nurse* 85, no. 6 (1989): 29-31.

231. Atkinson, Brian R. *Effect of Father Absenteeism on the Behaviour and Attitudes of Male Children between Eight and Sixteen Years of Age.* Calgary, AB: Boys' Clubs of Calgary, 1971.

232. Atkinson, Tom et al. *Physical Status and Perceived Health Quality.* Downsview, ON: York University, Institute for Behavioural Research, 1980.

233. Atlantic Provinces Education Foundation. *Education Indicators for Atlantic Canada.* Halifax, NS: The Foundation, 1996.

234. Attemeyer, Bob. "Marching in Step: A Psychological Explanation of State Terror." *Sciences* 28, no. 2 (1988): 30-38.

235. Baer, Douglas E., and Ronald D. Lambert. "Education and Support for Dominant Ideology." *Canadian Review of Sociology and Anthropology* 19, no. 2 (1982): 173-95.

236. Baer, Douglas E., and Ronald D. Lambert. "The Politics of Canadian Social Scientists: A Reply to Guimond and Palmer." *Canadian Review of Sociology and Anthropology* 26, no. 2 (1994): 46- 69.

237. Baker, Maureen. *Tobacco Smoking.* Current Issue Review, Ottawa, ON: Canada Library of Parliament, Research Branch, 1986.

238. Barrie, Lawrence Duncan. "An Examination of Social Workers' Attitudes towards the Issue of Legal and Civil Rights of Psychiatric Patients." M.S.W. thesis, University of Windsor, 1980.

239. Barron, Robert F. "Attitudes of Members of Educational Interest Groups towards the School Placement of Exceptional Children." Ph.D. diss., University of Alberta, 1979.

240. Baseline Market Research, and Nova Scotia. Priorities and Planning Secretariat. *Public Attitude Study of the Future of Nova Scotia.* Halifax, NS: Nova Scotia Priorities and Planning Secretariat, 1994.

241. Baseline Market Research, and Prince Edward Island. Advisory Council on the Status of Women. *Health Care Survey for Prince Edward Island: Final Report.* Fredericton, NB: Baseline Market Research, 1988.

242. Baudoin, Jean-Louis et al. *Toward a Canadian Advisory Council on Biomedical Ethics: Study Paper.* Ottawa, ON: Law Reform Commission of Canada, 1990.

243. Beasley, Richard et al. *Canada Youth and AIDS Study: New Brunswick Report*. Kingston, ON: Queen's University, 1988.

244. Beck, Kirk A. et al. "Knowledge, Compliance, and Attitudes of Teachers toward Mandatory Child Abuse Reporting in British Columbia." *Canadian Journal of Education* 19 (Winter 1994): 15-29.

245. Benoit, Cecelia. "Uneasy Partners: Midwives and Their Clients." *Canadian Journal of Sociology* 12, no. 3 (1987): 275-84.

246. Bergsgaard, Michael D. "Supervision of Mid-Career Teachers: Perceptions May Be the Key to Productivity." *Education Canada* 29, no. 3 (1989): 22-27.

247. Bickenbach, Jerome E. "Lawyers, Law Professors, and Racism in Ontario." *Queen's Quarterly* 96, no. 3 (1989): 585-98.

248. Bienvenue, Rita M. "Participation in an Educational Innovation: Enrollments in French Immersion Programs." *Canadian Journal of Sociology* 11, no. 4 (1986): 363-77.

249. Black, Ken. "Only New Attitudes Can Cure $40 Billion Drug Habit (Ontario)." *Canadian Speeches* 3, no. 6 (1989): 26-32.

250. Blackmore, G. C. "Study of the Relationship of Attitude towards School with Academic Achievement in High School." Master's thesis, University of Guelph, 1975.

251. Blume, Delorys et al. "Challenger 10 and Our Schoolchildren: Reflections on the Catastrophe." *Death Studies* 10, no. 2 (1986): 95-118.

252. Booth, Alan, and John N. Edwards. "Fathers: The Invisible Parent." *Sex Roles* 6, no. 3 (1980): 445-56.

253. Bordeleau, G., and L. M. Desjardins. *Vocational Attitudes of Franco Ontarian Students - Grades 12 and 13, 1974-1975 (abridged version); A Venir des etudiants Franco Ontariens 12 et 13 annees, 1974-1975 (version abregee)*. Toronto: Ontario Advisory Council for Franco-Ontarian Affairs, 1976.

254. Bouchard, Louise et al. "Selective Abortion: A New Moral Order? Consensus and Debate in the Medical Community." *International Journal of Health Services* 25, no. 1 (1995): 65-84.

255. Bourgon, Michele. "When Twenty Years Separate Us . . . Reflections of a Female Professor of Social Work; Quand vingt ans nous separent . . . Reflexion d'une professeure en travail social." *Canadian Social Work Review* 5 (Winter 1988): 108-15.

256. Boyd-Withers, C., and M. Protz. *Health Concerns of Ontarians.* Planning and Development Research, Working Paper, 89-10. Toronto, ON: TV Ontario, 1990.

257. Bradford, Brenda. *Criminal Justice Survey, 1995: A Prince Edward Island Study of Public Opinion Related to Criminal Justice.* Charlottetown, PEI: Prince Edward Island Health and Community Services Agency, 1995.

258. Bridges, J. S. "College Females' Perceptions of Adult Roles and Occupational Fields for Women: Abstract." *Canadian Home Economics Journal* 38, no. 1 (1988): 39.

259. British Columbia. Corrections Branch. *Beliefs, Goals, and Strategies.* Victoria, BC: Ministry of the Attorney General, Corrections Branch, 1986.

260. British Columbia. Mathematics Assessment Contract Team. *The 1985 British Columbia Mathematics Assessment: General Report.* Victoria, BC: Ministry of Education, Student Assessment Branch, 1985.

261. British Columbia. Ministry of Education. Student Assessment Branch. *1988 B.C. Reading and Written Expression Assessment.* Victoria, BC: The Ministry, 1989.

262. Brown, Marquessa. "Nursing Assistants' Behavior toward the Institutionalized Elderly." *Quarterly: A Journal of Long Term Care* 24, no. 1 (1988): 16-18.

263. Buchanan, Alan G. "Education and Ethnic Attitudes: Some Observations on Anglophones in New Brunswick." *Canadian Ethnic Studies* 19, no. 2 (1987): 110-16.

264. Canada. Department of National Health and Welfare. *The PAL Smoking Prevention Program: An Active Learning Approach to Attitudes, Ideas and Life Skills for 11 to 13 Year Olds.* Ottawa, ON: The Department, 1988.

265. Canada. Department of National Health and Welfare et al. *Summary Report Canada Health Attitudes and Behaviours Survey 9, 12 and 15 Year Olds 1984-85.* Ottawa, ON: The Department, 1985.

266. Canada. Department of National Health and Welfare. Health Services Branch, and Tacon. P. H. *Comparison of Attitudes towards the Effects of Smoking and Personality Variables of Smokers and Non-Smokers in a Population of University Students.* Ottawa, ON: Department of National Health and Welfare, 1972.

267. Canada. Department of National Health and Welfare. Health Services and Promotion Branch. *PAL Smoking Prevention Program: Program Introduction and Methodology - Lesson Plans and Background Notes - An Active Learning Approach to Attitudes, Ideas and Life Skills for 11 to 13 Year Olds.* Ottawa, ON: The Branch, 1986.

268. Canada. Federal-Provincial Conference of Health Ministers et al. *Nursing: Community-Related Personnel, Attitudes and Projects: A Commissioned Paper to the Community Health Centre Project.* Ottawa, ON: The Conference, 1974.

269. Canada. Health and Welfare Canada. *The Active Health Report on Alcohol, Tobacco and Marijuana.* Ottawa, ON: Health and Welfare Canada, 1989.

270. Canada. Health and Welfare Canada. *The Active Health Report on Seniors.* Ottawa, ON: Health and Welfare Canada, 1989.

271. Canada. Health and Welfare Canada. *National Survey on Drinking and Driving, 1988: Overview Report.* Ottawa, ON: Health and Welfare Canada, 1989.

272. Canada. Health and Welfare Canada. *Perspectives on Canada's Health Promotion Survey, 1985.* Ottawa, ON: Health and Welfare Canada, 1987.

273. Canada. Women's Bureau. *When I Grow Up: Career Expectations and Aspirations of Canadian Schoolchildren: A Pilot Project Undertaken for the Women's Bureau of Labour Canada.* Ottawa, ON: Labour Canada, 1986.

274. Cassie, J. R. Bruce. *Housing Mentally Retarded Students in a Regular School: An Evaluation of Attitudes and Practices Associated with Housing Two Classes of Mentally Retarded Students in Grimsby Central School.* Toronto, ON: Ontario Ministry of Education, 1977.

275. Catton, Katherine et al. *Adolescent Beliefs and Practices regarding the Law of Minors' Medical Consent: A Pilot Study.* Toronto, ON: University of Toronto, Centre for Urban and Community Studies, 1980.

276. Chandler, David B. *Capital Punishment in Canada: A Sociological Study of Repressive Law*. Toronto, ON: McClelland and Stewart, 1976.

277. Chandrasena, Ranjith. "Culture and Clinical Psychiatry." *Psychiatric Journal of the University of Ottawa* 8, no. 1 (1983): 16-19.

278. Chappell, Nenna L., and Nina Lee Colwill. "Medical Schools As Agents of Professional Socialization." *Canadian Review of Sociology and Anthropology* 18, no. 1 (1981): 67-81.

279. Charette, André. *Special Study on Adults with an Activity Limitation*. Canada Health Promotion Directorate, Technical Report Series. Ottawa, ON: Supply and Services Canada, 1988.

280. Cheng, M., and Sylvia Larter. *Study of Returning Students, Part II: The Attitudes of Principals, Guidance Counsellors, Teachers and Students to Returning Students*. Report, no. 149. Toronto, ON: Board of Education, 1978.

281. Christian, L. M. C. "Parental Attitudes toward Family Life and Sex Education in Prince Edward Island." M.Sc. thesis, University of Guelph, Department of Family Studies, 1975.

282. Clement, R. et al. "Inter-Ethnic Contact: Attitudinal Consequences." *Canadian Journal of Behavioural Science* 9, no. 3 (1977): 205-15.

283. Clifton, Rodney A. et al. "Effects of Ethnicity and Sex on Teachers' Expectations of Junior High School Students." *Sociology of Education* 59, no. 1 (1986): 58-67.

284. Cohen, Saul. *Treating Alcohol Problems*. Regina, SK: Saskatchewan Alcohol and Drug Abuse Commission, 1989.

285. Contemporary Research Centre. *Report of a Study on Public Attitudes, Opinions and Behaviour in Relation to the Ontario Legal Aid Plan*. Toronto, ON: The Centre, 1974.

286. Cowan, Douglas Stewart. "Teacher Attitude and Involvement in Outdoor Education." Master's thesis, University of Alberta, Faculty of Physical Education, 1972.

287. Crispino, L. et al. *Concerns and Attitudes of Probation Officers*. Toronto, ON: Ministry of Correctional Services, Planning and Research, 1977.

288. Crocker, Robert K. *Student Aspirations and Attitudes in the First Year of the Revised High School Program*. St. John's, NF: Memorial University of Newfoundland, Institute for Educational Research and Development, 1983.

289. Cruttenden, Kathleen Robertson. "Policy Analysis of Ontario's Long-Term Care Reform: Based on Moral Political Theory, Knowledge and Experience of Caregivers and Planners." Ph.D. diss., University of Waterloo, 1996.

290. Cumberland, Jennifer, and Edward Zamble. "General and Specific Measures of Attitudes toward Early Release of Criminal Offenders." *Canadian Journal of Behavioural Science* 24, no. 4 (1992): 442-55.

291. Cunningham, Harry A. *Teacher Attitudes to Environmental Education*. Winnipeg, MB: Manitoba Department of Renewable Resources, and Transportation Services, 1976.

292. Dalhouse, Marie, and James S. Frideres. "Intergenerational Congruency: The Role of the Family in Political Attitudes of Youth." *Journal of Family Issues* 17, no. 2 (1996): 227-48.

293. D'Arcy, Carl, and Joan Brockman. "Public Rejection of the Ex-Mental Patient: Are Attitudes Changing?" *Canadian Review of Sociology and Anthropology* 14, no. 1 (1977): 68-80.

294. Data Laboratories Research Consultants. *Report on a Survey of Canadians' Attitudes towards Education and Knowledge*. Montreal, PQ: The Consultants, 1978.

295. David, Robert K. *An Action Plan for School Improvement: Summary of Attitude Surveys in the County of Lacombe*. Edmonton, AB: Alberta Education, 1986.

296. Day, Elaine Mellen et al. *The B.C. French Immersion Assessment, 1987: General Report*. Victoria, BC: Province of British Columbia, Ministry of Education, Student Assessment Branch, 1988.

297. Dear, Michael et al. "Economic Cycles and Mental Health Care Policy: An Examination of the Macro-Context for Social Service Planning." *Social Science and Medicine* 13C, no. 1 (1979): 43-53.

298. Decision Making Information Canada Ltd. *Foster Care in Alberta: An Attitude Survey*. Edmonton, AB: Alberta Health and Social Development, 1974.

299. Defoe, Tracy A. *English as a Second Language Teachers and Culture: An Interview Study of Role Perceptions.* Vancouver, BC: Educational Research Institute of British Columbia, 1986.

300. Deitch, Patricia Karen. "Adolescent Attitudes and Knowledge toward Weight Control and Related Variables: Possible Segmentation Criteria for a Social Market." Master's thesis, University of Guelph, 1977.

301. DeKeseredy, Walter S., and Brian D. MacLean. "Exploring the Gender, Race, and Class Dimensions of Victimization: A Left Realist Critique of the Canadian Urban Victimization Survey." *International Journal of Offender Therapy and Comparative Criminology* 35, no. 2 (1991): 143-61.

302. Dekker, Barbara. "Principals and Teacher-Librarians -- Their Roles and Attitudes regarding School Libraries: Results of a Survey of Elementary Schools in Ontario." *School Libraries in Canada* 9, no. 2 (1989): 32-37.

303. Del Colombo, Marco. "Police: Male Police Officers Attitudes towards their Female Counterparts in the Windsor Police Services." Ph.D. diss., University of Windsor, 1995.

304. Denton, Frank T. et al. "Constituencies of Adult Education Programs: Similarities and Differences among Age Groups and Other Components of the Population." *The Canadian Journal of Education* 15, no. 1 (1990): 72-90.

305. DeVries, Brian, and Lawrence J. Walker. "Conceptual/Integrative Complexity and Attitudes toward Capital Punishment." *Personality and Social Psychology Bulletin* 13 (December 1987): 448-57.

306. DeVries, Brian, and Lawrence J. Walker. "Moral Reasoning and Attitudes toward Capital Punishment." *Developmental Psychology* 22 (July 1986): 509-13.

307. Dolan, Rob et al. "Survey of Knowledge and Attitudes with Regard to AIDS among Grade 7 and 8 Students in Ottawa-Carleton." *Canadian Journal of Public Health* 81, no. 2 (1990): 135-38.

308. Domino, George, and Antoon A. Leenaaro. "Attitudes toward Suicide: A Comparison of Canadian and U.S. College Students." *Suicide and Life Threatening Behaviour* 19, no. 2 (1989): 160-72.

309. Doob, Anthony N., and Julian V. Roberts. "Social Psychology, Social Attitudes, and Attitudes toward Sentencing." *Canadian Journal of Behavioural Science* 16, no. 4 (1984): 269-80.

310. Dore, Kathryn, and John Hoey. "Smoking Practices, Knowledge and Attitudes regarding Smoking of University Hospital Nurses." *Canadian Journal of Public Health* 79, no. 3 (1988): 170-74.

311. Doyle, James Allen. "A Study of the Relationship between Mental Health, Field Dependency and Attitudes toward the Female's Role." Ph.D. diss., University of Saskatchewan, 1974.

312. Dussart, C. et al. *Longitudinal Study of the Structure of Beliefs in Social Marketing: A Cross Comparison of Youth Attitudes towards Alcohol, Tobacco, and Marijuana in Canada.* Working Paper, 86-58. Ottawa, ON: University of Ottawa, Faculty of Administration, 1986.

313. Earl, L. M., and R. G. Stennett. *Survey of Student's Attitudes towards Physical and Health Education: Saunders Secondary School, January 1983.* Toronto, ON: Ontario Ministry of Education, 1983.

314. Edwards, Nancy, and Kathleen MacMillan. "Tobacco Use and Ethnicity: The Existing Data Gap." *Canadian Journal of Public Health* 81, no. 1 (1990): 32-36.

315. Einsiedel, Edna F. "Mental Maps of Science: Knowledge and Attitudes among Canadian Adults." *International Journal of Public Opinion Research* 6, no. 1 (1994): 35-44.

316. Erickson, Patricia G. "The Defence Lawyer's Role in Juvenile Court: An Empirical Investigation." *University of Toronto Law Journal* 24, no. 2 (1974): 126-48.

317. Fattah, Ezat Abdel. *Canadian Public and the Death Penalty - A Study of a Social Attitude.* Ottawa, ON: Department of the Solicitor General, Research and Systems Development Branch, 1975.

318. Finlay, J. Richard. "The Strange, Skeptical Mood of the Campus: A Poll Uncovers Surprising Attitudes--and Heroes--Among Students." *Saturday Night* 94, no. 8 (1979): 35-40.

319. Fleming, Stephen, and Isabel Brown. "Impact of a Death Education Program for Nurses in a Long-Term Care Hospital." *Gerontologist* 23, no. 2 (1983): 192-95.

320. Foster, Mary Kathleen. "Attitudes of Canadian Physicians in the United States: The Role of Selection and Socialization." Ph.D. diss., Columbia University, 1976.

321. Frankel, B. Gail, and W. E. Hewitt. "Religion and Well-Being among Canadian University Students: The Role of Faith Groups on Campus." *Journal for the Scientific Study of Religion* 33, no. 1 (1994): 62-73.

322. Freeman, Milton M. R. "Anthropologists and Social Involvement in Canada." *Human Organization* 33, no. 4 (1974): 391-93.

323. Frideres, James S., and Jay E. Goldstein. "Jewish-Gentile Intermarriage: Definitions and Consequences." *Social Compass* 21, no. 1 (1974): 69-84.

324. Fulton, Patricia Lynne. "Social and Personal Values and Attitudes of Newfoundland Lightkeepers: A Dyadic Life History of a Married Couple." Ph.D. diss., Memorial University of Newfoundland, 1989.

325. Gagan, David. "'The Prose of Life': Literary Reflections of the Family, Individual." *Journal of Social History* 9, no. 3 (1976): 367-81.

326. Gardner, R. C., and L. M. Lysynchuk. "Role of Aptitude, Attitudes, Motivation, and Language Use on Second-Language Acquisition and Retention." *The Canadian Journal of Behavioural Science* 22, no. 3 (1990): 254-70.

327. Genesee, Fred. "Beyond Bilingualism: Social Psychological Studies of French Immersion Programs in Canada." *Canadian Journal of Behavioural Science* 16, no. 4 (1984): 338-52.

328. Gilbert, Sid, and Bruce Orok. "School Leavers." *Canadian Social Trends* (Autumn 1993): 2-7.

329. Globerman, Judith. "Free Enterprise, Professional Ideology, and Self-Interest: An Analysis of Resistance by Canadian Physicians to Universal Health Insurance." *Journal of Health & Social Behavior* 31 (March 1990): 11-27.

330. Godfreyson, John Ernst. *An Investigation of Attitudes towards the Use of Computer Games and Simulations in the Primary / Elementary Classroom Environment.* ERIBC Reports, no. 84:7. Vancouver, BC: Educational Research Institute of British Columbia, 1984.

331. Gold, Marc. "Of Rights and Roles: The Supreme Court and the Charter." *University of British Columbia Law Review* 23, no. 3 (1989): 507-30.

332. Goldman, Juliette G. G., and Ronald J. Goldman. "Children's Perceptions of Parents and Their Roles: A Cross-National Study in Australia, England, North America, and Sweden." *Sex Roles* 9, no. 7 (1983): 791-812.

333. Goodwin, Patrick Charles. "A Sociological Study of the Effects of Social Class on Parental Attitudes toward Their Children." Master's thesis, University of Windsor, 1981.

334. Gordon, Robert et al. "The Right to Refuse Treatment: Commonwealth Developments and Issues." *International Journal of Law and Psychiatry* 6, no. 1 (1983): 57-73.

335. Gorman, M. C. "Some Attitudes and Perceptions towards Death and Dying." Master's thesis, University of Guelph, 1975.

336. Gottesfeld, Leslie, and M. Johnson. "Conservation, Territory and Traditional Beliefs: An Analysis of Gitksan and Wet'suwet'en Subsistence, Northwest British Columbia, Canada." *Human Ecology* 22, no. 4 (1994): 443-65.

337. Gow, Christina M., and J. Ivan Williams. "Nurses' Attitudes toward Death and Dying: A Causal Interpretation." *Social Science and Medicine* 11, no. 3 (1977): 191-98.

338. Grindstaff, Carl F. "The Canadian Pharmacist and Family Planning." *Family Planning Perspectives* 9, no. 2 (1977): 81-84.

339. Guimond, Serge et al. "Education, Academic Program and Intergroup Attitudes." *Canadian Review of Sociology and Anthropology* 26, no. 2 (1989): 193-216.

340. Guimond, Serge. "Encounter and Metamorphosis: The Impact of Military Socialization on Professional Values." *Applied Psychology: An International Review* 44, no. 3 (1995): 251-75.

341. Guimond, Serge, and Douglas L. Palmer. "Type of Academic Training and Causal Attributions for Social Problems." *European Journal of Social Psychology* 20, no. 1 (1990): 61-75.

342. Haddad, Tony, and Lawrence Lam. "Canadian Families-Men's Involvement in Family Work: A Case Study of Immigrant Men in Toronto." *International Journal of Comparative Sociology* 29, no. 3-4 (1988): 269-81.

343. Hagan, John. "Law, Order and Sentencing: A Study of Attitude in Action." *Sociometry* 38, no. 3 (1975): 374-84.

344. Hagan, John, and Nancy O'Donnel. "Sexual Stereotyping and Judicial Sentencing: A Legal Test of the Sociological Wisdom." *Canadian Journal of Sociology* 3, no. 3 (1978): 309-19.

345. Hall, David Ray. "Reproduction Individualism and Divorce: An Examination of Attitudes and Marriage Dissolution in Canada." Ph.D. diss., University of Western Ontario, 1993.

346. Harrison, Trevor, and Harvey Krahn. "Populism and the Rise of the Reform Party in Alberta." *Canadian Review of Sociology and Anthropology* 32, no. 2 (1995): 127-50.

347. Hass, Jack, and William Shaffir. *Becoming Doctors: The Adoption of a Cloak of Competence*. Greenwich, CT: JAI Press, 1987.

348. Haynes, Dave. "Prevention Messages Heard but Not Heeded (Young Adults Change Attitudes about Drinking but Not Behavior)." *The Journal* 19, no. 4 (1990): 3.

349. Head, W., and D. H. Clairmont. *Royal Commission on the Donald Marshall, Jr., Prosecution*. Vol. 4: *Discrimination against Blacks in Nova Scotia: The Criminal Justice System*. Halifax, NS: The Commission, 1989.

350. Herberg, Dorothy Chave. "Issues in Multicultural Child Welfare: Working with Families Originating in Traditional Societies." *Social Work Papers* 17 (Summer 1983): 45-57.

351. Hetherington, Robert W. "Response to Innovation: The Problem-Oriented System in a Mental Health Setting." *Canadian Review of Sociology and Anthropology* 21 (May 1984): 202-30.

352. Hildebrandt, Kai et al. "The Windsor Small Claims Court: An Empirical Study of Plaintiffs and Their Attitudes." *Windsor Yearbook of Access to Justice* 2 (1982): 87-123.

353. Hobart, Charles W. "Attitudes toward Illegitimacy in Alberta." *Canadian Journal of Sociology* 1, no. 3 (1975): 263-75.

354. Hobart, Charles W. "Attitudes toward Parenthood among Canadian Young People." *Journal of Marriage and the Family* 35, no. 1 (1973): 71-82.

355. Holmes, Mark, and Edward A. Wynne. *Making the School an Effective Community: Belief, Practice and Theory in School Administration*. New York, NY: Falmer Press, 1989.

356. Hunsberger, Bruce. "The Religiosity of College Students: Stability and Change over Years at University." *Journal for the Scientific Study of Religion* 17, no. 2 (1978): 159-64.

357. Isherwood, Geoffrey B. "College Choice: A Survey of English-Speaking High School Students in Quebec." *The Canadian Journal of Education* 16, no. 1 (1991): 72-81.

358. Jackson, Margaret A. *Judicial Attitudes towards Community Sentencing Options.* Toronto, ON: Ontario Ministry of Correctional Services, 1982.

359. Jaenen, Cornelius J. "The Impact of Ideological Issues on Public Schools and Public Policy." *Journal of Comparative Sociology* 2 (1974): 72-88.

360. Jaffe, Peter G. et al. "Promoting Changes in Attitudes and Understanding of Conflict Resolution among Child Witnesses of Family Violence." *Canadian Journal of Behavioural Science* 18, no. 4 (1986): 356-66.

361. Jaffe, Peter G. et al. "Youth's Knowledge and Attitudes about the Young Offenders Act: Does Anyone Care What They Think?" *Canadian Journal of Criminology* 29 (July 1987): 309-16.

362. Jeroski, Sharon. *The 1988 British Columbia Assessment of Reading and Written Expression: Technical Report.* Victoria, BC: Ministry of Education, Student Assessment Branch, 1989.

363. Jones, Pauline A. "The Validity of Traditional-Modern Attitude Measures." *Journal of Cross-Cultural Psychology* 8, no. 2 (1977): 207-39.

364. Jonsson, Barbara. "An Investigation of the Long Term Stability and Predictability of Children's Social Characteristics and Parents' Child Rearing Attitudes and Practices." Master's thesis, University of Calgary, 1977.

365. Kallen, Evelyn. "Academics, Politics and Ethnics: University Opinion on Canadian Ethnic Studies." *Canadian Ethnic Studies* 13, no. 2 (1981): 112-23.

366. Kannampadam, Joseph T. "An Investigation of Attitudes of Secondary School Students in Newfoundland toward the Grade Ten Social Studies Course: Canadian Society, Issues and Concerns." M.Ed. thesis, Memorial University of Newfoundland, 1978.

367. Kelner, Merrijoy, and Carolyn Rosenthal. "Postgraduate Medical Training, Stress, and Marriage." *Canadian Journal of Psychiatry* 31, no. 1 (1986): 22-24.

368. Kerr, Carolyn L., and Mona June Horrocks. "Knowledge, Values, Attitudes and Behavioural Intent of Nova Scotia Nurses towards AIDS and Patients with AIDS." *Canadian Journal of Public Health* 81, no. 2 (1990): 125-34.

369. Kim, Y. C. *Survey of Attitude and Knowledge Concerning Marijuana and its Uses among High School Students.* Regina, SK: Alcoholism Commission of Saskatchewan, Research Division, 1971.

370. Kirkwood, Kristian J. *Survey of Elementary and Secondary Pupils: Their Knowledge and Attitudes Concerning Canada.* London, ON: University of Western Ontario, Faculty of Education, 1983.

371. Klassen, Janice. *Health Foods: Report on Opinion Survey Conducted Summer 1986.* Ottawa, ON: Health and Welfare Canada, 1987.

372. Kornberg, Allan, and Harold D. Clarke. "Beliefs about Democracy and Satisfaction with Democratic Government: The Canadian Case." *Political Research Quarterly* 47, no. 3 (1994): 537.

373. Krishnan, Vijaya. "Abortion in Canada: Religious and Ideological Dimensions of Women's Attitudes." *Social Biology* 38, no. 3-4 (1991): 249-57.

374. Kurian, George. "Dynamics of Youth Attitudes in South Asian Families." *International Journal of Contemporary Sociology* 23, no. 1-2 (1986): 69-86.

375. Kurian, George, and Ratna Ghosh. "Changing Authority within the Context of Socialization in Indian Families." *Social Science* 53, no. 1 (1978): 24-32.

376. Laakso, D. L. "Nutrition Practices and Health Beliefs of a Group of Women." Master's thesis, University of Guelph, 1986.

377. Labun, Evelyn. "Vietnamese Woman in Canada: Learning about a Different Perspective on Health." *The Canadian Nurse* 84, no. 8 (1988): 49-50.

378. Lachapelle, Diane et al. "Dental Health Education for Adolescents: Assessing Attitude and Knowledge following Two Educational Approaches." *Canadian Journal of Public Health* 80, no. 5 (1989): 339-44.

379. Laing, Lory, and P. Krishman. "First-Marriage Decrement: Tables for Males and Females in Canada, 1961-1966." *Canadian Review of Sociology and Anthropology* 13, no. 2 (1976): 217-28.

380. Lambert, Ronald D., and James E. Curtis. "Education, Economic Dissatisfaction, and Nonconfidence in Canadian Social Institutions." *Canadian Review of Sociology and Anthropology* 16, no. 1 (1979): 47-59.

381. Lambert, Ronald D., and James E. Curtis. "Quebecois and English Canadian Opposition to Racial and Religious Intermarriage, 1968-1983." *Canadian Ethnic Studies* 16, no. 2 (1984): 30-46.

382. Lambert, Wallace E. "The Fate of Old-Country Values in a New Land: A Cross-National Study of Child Rearing." *Canadian Psychology* 28, no. 1 (1987): 9-20.

383. Land, Mary. "Librarians' Image and Users' Attitudes to Reference Interviews." *Canadian Library Journal* 45, no. 1 (1988): 15-20.

384. Larter, Sylvia et al. *Writing with Microcomputers in the Elementary Grades: Processes, Roles, Attitudes, and Products.* Education and Technology Series. Toronto, ON: Ontario Ministry of Education, 1987.

385. Lee, Linda E. *Teacher Attitudes towards Educational Issues.* Research, no. 84-07. Winnipeg, MB: Manitoba Department of Education, Planning and Research Branch, 1984.

386. Leenaars, Antoon A. "Suicide and the Continental Divide." *Archives of Suicide Research* 1, no. 1 (1995): 39-58.

387. Lenton, Rhonda L. "Techniques of Child Discipline and Abuse by Parents." *Canadian Review of Sociology and Anthropology* 27, no. 2 (1990): 157-85.

388. Lero, D. S., and Susan de Rijcke-Lollis. *Early Childhood Educators and Private Home Day Care Providers Knowledge: Attitudes and Experiences Related to Child Abuse.* Toronto, ON: Ministry of Community and Social Services, Children's Services Division, 1978.

389. Leung, Jupian J., and Stephen F. Foster. "Cultural Differences in Attitudes toward Teachers and Learning: Chinese-Canadian and Non-Chinese Canadian Children." *Canadian Ethnic Studies* 17, no. 1 (1985): 90-97.

390. Lightman, Ernie S. "Professionalization, Bureaucratization, and Unionization in Social Work." *Social Service Review* 56, no. 1 (1982): 130-43.

391. Livingstone, D. W. *Public Attitudes toward Education in Ontario 1978 - The OISE Survey Report.* Toronto, ON: Ontario Institute for Studies in Education, 1978.

392. Livingstone, D. W. *Public Attitudes toward Education in Ontario 1978: The OISE Survey Report.* Toronto, ON: Ontario Ministry of Education, Research and Evaluation Branch, 1979.

393. Livingstone, D. W. et al. *Public Attitudes toward Education in Ontario 1982 - Fourth OISE Survey.* Toronto, ON: Ontario Institute for Studies in Education, 1983.

394. Livingstone, D. W., and D. Hart. *Public Attitudes toward Education in Ontario 1980 - Third OISE Survey.* Toronto, ON: Ontario Institute for Studies in Education, 1981.

395. Mackie, Marlene. "Sociology, Academia, and the Community: Maligned Within Invisible Without? " *Canadian Journal of Sociology* 1, no. 2 (1975): 203-21.

396. MacNamara, John Theodore, and John N. Edwards. *Attitudes to Learning French in the English-Speaking Schools of Quebec.* Quebec City, PQ: Quebec Official Publisher, 1973.

397. Macurdy, E. A., and M. J. Hollander. *Survey of Drinking Practices and Attitudes to Alcohol Use in British Columbia.* Vancouver, BC: British Columbia Alcohol and Drug Commission, Research and Planning Division, 1978.

398. Manitoba. Department of Education. Planning and Research Branch. *Public Attitudes to Education.* Winnipeg, MB: Manitoba Education, Planning and Research Branch, 1984.

399. Manitoba. Department of Health and Social Development. *Summary Report of Results - Alcohol and Drug Attitude and Information Survey.* Winnipeg, MB: Department of Health and Social Development, Correctional and Rehabilitative Services, 1976.

400. Manitoba. Manitoba Health. *Report of the Workplace Smoking Survey among Employees of Manitoba Health. January, 1987.* Winnipeg, MB: Manitoba Department of Health, 1987.

401. Marous, A. M. *Structure of Popular Beliefs about Alcoholism.* Toronto, ON: Addiction Research Foundation, 1980.

402. Marrow, N. R. "Parental Attitudes and Achievement Motivation in Children." Master's thesis, University of Guelph, Department of Agricultural Economics and Extension, 1973.

403. Massey, Barbara Jane. "A Survey of Counselor, Student, Teacher, Administrator, Parent, and School Trustee Attitudes and Factors Influencing Attitudes toward Present High School Counselling Services." Ph.D. diss., University of Alberta, 1973.

404. Matas, M. et al. "Mental Illness and the Media: An Assessment of Attitudes and Communication." *Canadian Journal of Psychiatry* 30, no. 1 (1985): 12-17.

405. McConnell, Harvey. "Research: Anti-Science Attitude Posing Real Threat." *The Journal* 18, no. 6 (1989): 3.

406. McDaniel, S. A. *Women and Family in the Later Years: Findings from the 1990 General Social Survey*. Research Discussion Paper, no. 84. Edmonton, AB: University of Alberta, Department of Sociology, 1991.

407. McGregor, A. J. "Smoking Attitudes and Behaviour of Student Nurses." Master's thesis, University of Guelph, 1984.

408. McInnes, David. "And Now - Consumerism!" *The Canadian Banker* 96 (July/August 1989): 6-9.

409. McNevin, Stephen H. et al. "Sex Role Ideology among Health Care Professionals." *Psychiatric Journal of the University of Ottawa* 10, no. 1 (1985): 21-23.

410. Meunier, Claude, and Alice Poznanska Parizeau. *Analysis on Public Opinion: Study of Royal Commission of Inquiry Briefs*. Montreal, PQ: University of Montreal, International Centre for Comparative Criminology, 1973.

411. Micco, Angela et al. "Case Manager Attitudes toward Client-Directed Care." *Journal of Case Management* 4, no. 3 (1995): 95-101.

412. Michaels, Evelyne. "Medical Advances, Positive Attitudes Brighten Future of Down's Children." *Canadian Medical Association Journal* 143, no. 6 (1990): 546-47, 549.

413. Millar, W. J. *Smoke in the Workplace: An Evaluation of Smoking Restrictions*. Ottawa, ON: Health and Welfare Canada, 1988.

414. Millson, Margaret et al. "AIDS-Related Knowledge, Attitudes and Behaviour in Injection Drug Users Attending a Toronto Treatment Facility." *Canadian Journal of Public Health* 81, no. 1 (1990): 46-49.

415. Moase, Reginald Beverly. "A Study of Educational Attitudes of a Sample of Candidates Seeking Teacher Certification in Ontario." Ph.D. diss., University of Toronto, 1978.

416. Molloy, David W. et al. "Treatment Preferences, Attitudes toward Advance Directives and Concerns about Health Care." *Humane Medicine* 7, no. 4 (1991): 285-90.

417. Moore, Barbara G. *Equity in Education: Gender Issues in the Use of Computers: A Review and Bibliography*. Review and Evaluation Bulletins, Education and Technology Series, v. 6, no. 1. Toronto, ON: Ontario Ministry of Education, 1986.

418. Moore, Robert J. "The Public's Perception of the Law and the Legal System: A Strategy for Research." *Windsor Yearbook of Access to Justice* 1 (1981): 214-29.

419. Moss, Lawrence G. "Social Correlates of Parental Attitudes toward Education in the City of St. John's." M.Ed. thesis, Memorial University of Newfoundland, 1973.

420. Moyer, Sharon, and Peter J. Carrington. *The Attitudes of Canadian Juvenile Justice Professionals towards the Young Offenders Act*. Programs Branch User Report, no. 1985-22. Ottawa, ON: Ministry of the Solicitor General, 1987.

421. Murphy, Raymond. "Teachers and the Evolving Structural Context of Economic and Political Attitudes in Quebec Society." *Canadian Review of Sociology and Anthropology* 18, no. 2 (1981): 157- 82.

422. Myers, Ted et al. *Men's Survey '90: A Toronto Venue-Based Survey of Gay and Bisexual Men and Their Knowledge, Attitudes, and Behaviour Related to HIV/AIDS*. Toronto, ON: AIDS Committee of Toronto, 1991.

423. Nagy, G. Philip, and Roslyn Klaiman. "Attitudes to and Impact of French Immersion: With Summaries in German and Spanish." *The Canadian Journal of Education* 13, no. 2 (1988): 263-76.

424. National Clearinghouse on Family Violence (Canada). Family Violence Prevention Division. *Promoting Changes in Attitudes and Understanding of Conflict Resolution among Child Witnesses of Family Violence*. Ottawa, ON: National Clearinghouse on Family Violence, 1986.

425. New Brunswick. Department of Solicitor General, and Baseline Market Research. *Public Attitude Survey: Crime, Safety and Policing Services in New Brunswick; New Brunswick Policing Study, Vol. III: Public Attitude Survey*. Fredericton, NB: Baseline Market Research, 1991.

426. Nicolson, Norman Page. "A Study of the Attitudes Parents Have toward Their Child's Elementary School and the Relationship of Those Attitudes to Religious Conviction, Social Mobility and Social Class." Ph.D. diss., Michigan State University, 1985.

427. Nixon, Mary, and L. R. Gue. "Women Administrators and Women Teachers: A Comparative Study." *Alberta Journal of Educational Research* 21, no. 1 (1975): 196-206.

428. Nogradi, George Steve. "An Analysis of Existing Relationships between the Administrative Processes and Organizational Commitment and Job Involvement of Recreational Staff Members within Mental Health Centres across Canada." Ph.D. diss., University of Oregon, 1978.

429. Norman, Ross M. G. *Special Study on the Relationship between Social Networks and Health Promoting Behaviours and Attitudes*. Technical Report Series. Ottawa, ON: Health and Welfare Canada, Health Promotion Directorate, 1988.

430. Northcott, Herbert C., and Linda Reutter. "Public Opinion regarding AIDS Policy: Fear of Contagion and Attitude toward Homosexual Relationships." *Canadian Journal of Public Health* 82, no. 2 (1991): 87-91.

431. Ontario. Addiction Research Foundation. *Police Attitudes toward Drinking - Driving Enforcement*. Toronto, ON: The Foundation, 1977.

432. Ontario. Health Disciplines Board. *Ontario. Annual Report. Health Disciplines Board; Denture Therapists Appeal Board*. Toronto, ON: Ministry of Health, 1989.

433. Ontario. Ministry of Education. *Science Is Happening Here: A Policy Statement for Science in the Primary and Junior Divisions*. Toronto, ON: The Ministry, 1988.

434. Ontario. Ministry of Education. Research and Evaluation Branch. *Public Opinions and Attitudes toward Education: 654 Personal Interviews.* Toronto, ON: The Branch, 1979.

435. Ontario. Ministry of Education, and The Canadian Gallup Poll Limited. *Attitudes of the Public towards Schools in Ontario.* Toronto, ON: Ontario Ministry of Education, 1979.

436. Ornstein, Michael D. *AIDS in Canada: Knowledge, Behaviour and Attitudes of Adults.* Toronto, ON: York University, Institute for Social Research, 1989.

437. Pancer, S. Mark et al. "Religions Orthodoxy and the Complexity of Thought about Religious and Nonreligious Issues." *Journal of Personality* 63, no. 2 (1995): 213-32.

438. Pannu, R. S., and J. R. Young. "Ethnic Schools in Three Canadian Cities: A Study in Multiculturalism." *Alberta Journal of Educational Research* 26, no. 4 (1980): 247-61.

439. Panther, Katherine J. et al. "Children's Reactions to a Community Economic Crisis: An Exploratory Analysis." *Sociological Studies of Child Development* 2 (1987): 225-42.

440. Papageorgiou, Y. Y., and A. J. Harrison. *Prevailing Social Attitudes toward Distributive Justice.* Hamilton, ON: McMaster University, Department of Economics, 1983.

441. Parakulam, George. *Promoting the Health of Albertans: A Study of Practices, Attitudes and Beliefs Impinging on Chronic Disease Prevention.* Edmonton, AB: Alberta Community and Occupational Health, 1987.

442. Parkin, M., and Ontario. Ministry of Education. *French Immersion Research Relevant to Decisions in Ontario.* Review and Evaluation Bulletins, Education and Technology Series, v. 8 no. 1. Toronto, ON: Ministry of Education, 1987.

443. Peacock, Susan. "Creative Thinking, Attitudes, Interests and Social Relationships of Students in an Open Programme School." Master's thesis, University of Toronto, 1973.

444. Perner, Darlene Elizabeth. *An Exploratory Study of the Behaviors and Attitudes of Regular Class Teachers towards Special Needs Pupils Integrated in Their Classes.* Vancouver, BC: Educational Research Institute of British Columbia, 1985.

445. Perry, Lind A., and Manitoba. Attorney General. Research, Planning and Evaluation Branch. *The Expansion of the Family Division of the Court of Queen's Bench: Feasibility Study.* Winnipeg, MB: Manitoba Attorney General, Research, Planning and Evaluation Branch, 1986.

446. Pierre, Karin Domnick. "The Workplace and Mental Health." *Canadian Home Economics Journal* 36 (1986): 52-55.

447. Pike, Robert. "Legal Access and the Incidence of Divorce in Canada: A Sociohistorical Analysis." *Canadian Review of Sociology and Anthropology* 12, no. 2 (1975): 115-33.

448. Pope, O. T., and P. Cincurak. *Teacher Education: A Review of the Literature, 1980-89 [and] N.B. Teachers' Attitudes toward Integration: Research Reports.* Fredericton, NB: New Brunswick School Research Consortium, 1990.

449. Prince Edward Island. Advisory Council on the Status of Women. *High School and Beyond: Choices and Attitudes: A Survey of Prince Edward Island Senior High School Students Concerning Course Selection, Career Planning, and the Roles of Women and Men in Society.* Report, no. 1. Charlottetown, PE: The Council, 1988.

450. Pyra, Joseph Frederick. "Characteristics and Attitudes of Modernity of Teacher Candidates in the Eastern and Western Regions of Canada." Ph.D. diss., University of Calgary, 1971.

451. Quality Control Research Inc et al. *Results of a Study among Albertan Adults and Teens on the Subject of AIDS and HIV Infection: Final Report; The Alberta AIDS Survey, December, 1987.* Edmonton, AB: Alberta Community and Occupational Health, 1988.

452. Quebec. Conseil superieur de l'education. *Learning for Real: Testimonies on the Stakes and Conditions for Quality Pupil Development: Summary of the 1984-1985 Annual Report of the State and Needs of Education in Quebec.* Quebec City, PQ: The Conseil, 1985.

453. Rabin, David L. et al. "The World Health Organization International Collaborative Study of Medical Care Utilization: A Summary of Methodological Studies and Preliminary Findings." *Social Science and Medicine* 8, no. 5 (1974): 255-62.

454. Rae-Grant, Quentin. "Family Violence Myths, Measures and Mandates." *Canadian Journal of Psychiatry* 28, no. 7 (1983): 505-12.

455. Ralph, Edwin. "Developing Professional Attributes among Student Teachers during Field Experience Programs." *Education Canada* 29, no. 1 (1989): 32-40.

456. Ramu, D. N., and Nicholas Javachis. "The Valuation of Children and Parenthood among the Voluntarily Childless and Parental Couples in Canada." *Journal of Comparative Family Studies* 17, no. 1 (1986): 99-116.

457. Randhawa, Bikker S., and Susan Korpan. *Dimensions of a Scale of Attitude toward the Learning of French as a Second Language and Their Correlates.* Information and Research Report. Saskatoon, SK: University of Saskatchewan, Education Research Resources Centre, 1972.

458. Raphael, Dennis. "Debunking the Semestering Myth." *Canadian Journal of Education* 11 (1986): 36-52.

459. Reid, Angus E. "The Development of Work-Related Attitudes and Behavior of Professional Recruits: A Test of the Functionalist Argument." *Journal of Health & Social Behavior* 20, no. 4 (1979): 338-51.

460. Reid, Angus E. "Socialization into the Professions: The Impact of Dental School Faculty on Students' Professional Orientations." *Canadian Review of Sociology and Anthropology* 18, no. 1 (1981): 48-66.

461. Reimer, Samuel H. "A Look at Cultural Effects on Religiosity: A Comparison between the United States and Canada." *Journal for the Scientific Study of Religion* 34, no. 4 (1995): 445-57.

462. Richer, Stephen. "Programme Composition and Educational Plans." *Sociology of Education* 47, no. 3 (1974): 337-53.

463. Richer, Stephen. "Schooling and the Gendered Subject: An Exercise in Planned Social Change." *Canadian Review of Sociology and Anthropology* 25, no. 1 (1988): 98-107.

464. Richman, Alex et al. "Prevention of Alcohol-Related Problems." *Drug and Alcohol Dependence* 20, no. 1 (1987): 9-37.

465. Roberts, J. V. *Sexual Assault Legislation in Canada, an Evaluation: Sentencing Patterns in Cases of Sexual Assault.* Report, no. 3. Ottawa, ON: Department of Justice, Policy, Programs and Research Sector, Research Section, 1990.

466. Roberts, Julian. "Early Release from Prison: What Do the Canadian Public Really Think?" *Canadian Journal of Criminology* 30, no. 3 (1988): 231-49.

467. Roberts, Julian V. *Public Knowledge of Crime and Justice: An Inventory of Canadian Findings*. Technical Report, TR1994-15e. Ottawa, ON: Department of Justice, Corporate Management, Policy and Program Sector, Research, Statistics and Evaluation Directorate, 1994.

468. Robertson, J. Bruce. *What's the Point: Judicial Objectives in Sentencing*. Programs Branch User Report, no. 1985-37. Ottawa, ON: Ministry of the Solicitor General, 1987.

469. Rooke, Patricia T., and R. L. Schnell. "Child Welfare in English Canada, 1920-1948." *Social Service Review* 55, no. 3 (1981): 484-506.

470. Rosenbaum, P. D., and J. Bursten. *Special Study on Labour Force Groups*. Technical Report Series. Ottawa, ON: Health and Welfare Canada, Health Promotion Directorate, 1988.

471. Rupert, Constance Elizabeth. "Attitudes in Social Work and the Multi-Problem Family: A Case Study." Master's thesis, Simon Fraser University, 1974.

472. Ryan, Doris W., and Edward S. Hickcox. *Redefining Teacher Evaluation: An Analysis of Practices, Policies, and Teacher Attitudes*. Research in Education Series, 10. Toronto, ON: Ontario Institute for Studies in Education, 1980.

473. Sargenia, Garry D. "Leadership Attitudes of Social Work Students." Master's thesis, University of Calgary, 1974.

474. Saskatchewan. University Program Review Panel. *Looking at Saskatchewan Universities: Programs, Governance, and Goals: Report*. Regina, SK: The Panel, 1993.

475. Savard, Catherine, and Louise Langelier-Biron. *Female Perpetrators of Serious Offenses*. Programs Branch User Report, no. 1986-16. Ottawa, ON: Ministry of the Solicitor General, 1986.

476. Schneider, Barry H. et al. *The Social Adjustment of Gifted Children in Ontario Schools*. Toronto, ON: Ontario Ministry of Education, 1987.

477. Schneider, Frank W. et al. "In Favour of Coeducation: The Educational Attitudes of Students from Coeducational and Single-Sex High Schools: With Summaries in French, German and Spanish." *The Canadian Journal of Education* 13, no. 4 (1988): 479-96.

478. Schneider, Frank W., and Larry M. Coutts. "Teacher Orientations towards Masculine and Feminine: Role of Sex of Teacher and Sex Composition of School." *Canadian Journal of Behavioural Science* 11, no. 2 (1979): 99-111.

479. Schriever, Silvia H. "Comparison of Beliefs and Practices of Ethnic Viet and Lao Hmong concerning Illness, Healing, Death and Mourning: Implications for Hospice Care with Refugees in Canada." *Journal of Palliative Care* 6, no. 1 (1990): 42-49.

480. Segall, Alexander. "Age Differences in Lay Conceptions of Health and Self-Care Responses to Illness." *Canadian Journal on Aging* 6, no. 1 (1987): 47-65.

481. Semple, S. J. "Generational Model of Child Care: Intergenerational Attitudes toward Child-Rearing Practices." M.Sc. thesis, University of Guelph, 1985.

482. Serge, Guimond, and Douglas L. Palmer. "The Politics of Canadian Social Scientists: A Comment on Baer and Lambert." *Canadian Review of Sociology and Anthropology* 31, no. 2 (1994): 184-95.

483. Shapiro, M. F. et al. "Residents Experiences in, and Attitudes toward the Care of Persons with AIDS in Canada, France, and the United-States." *JAMA - Journal of the American Medical Association* 268, no. 4 (1992): 510-15.

484. Sharman, Rex G. "Student Satisfaction and Achievement Related to Organizational Structure: A Study on Semestering in Junior High." *Education Canada* 29, no. 3 (1989): 28-35.

485. Silberstein, Edward B., and C. Jane Scott. "An Evaluation of Undergraduate Family Care Programs." *Journal of Community Health* 3, no. 4 (1978): 369-79.

486. Simmons, Alan B., and Jean E. Turner. "The Socializations of Sex-Roles and Fertility Ideals: A Study of Two Generations in Toronto." *Journal of Comparative Family Studies* 7, no. 2 (1976): 255-71.

487. Skinner, Shirley et al. *Corrections: An Historical Perspective of the Saskatchewan Experience.* Canadian Plains Reports, 4. Regina, SK: Canadian Plains Research Center, 1981.

488. Smith, Betty Stafford, and Mary G. Alton Mackey. "Study of Consumer Knowledge, Attitudes, and Behavior in a Selected Group of Quebec CEGEP (Colleges d'enseignement general et professionel) Students." _Canadian Home Economics Journal_ 39, no. 4 (1989): 168-74.

489. Smith, Carol E. "Perceptions of Nursing Students from Two Northern Latitudes: Comparing Cultural Patterns and Norms." _International Journal of Comparative Sociology_ 28, no. 3-4 (1987): 236-43.

490. Smith, Elliot R. et al. "Law, Order and Sentencing." _Sociometry_ 39, no. 3 (1976): 288-92.

491. Smith, G., and D. Goodwillie. _Attitudes towards University_. Barometer, 4. Guelph, ON: University of Guelph, Office of the Provost, 1978.

492. Smythe, P. C. "Attitude, Aptitude, and Type of Instructional Programme in Second Language Acquisition." _Canadian Journal of Behavioural Science_ 4 (1972): 307-21.

493. Snider, Earle L. "The Elderly and Their Doctors." _Social Science and Medicine_ 14, no. 6A (1980): 527-31.

494. Spence, Gary. _The Educational Effects of Word Processors: County of Lacombe No. 14_. Edmonton, AB: Alberta Education, 1986.

495. Stanwick, Richard S. et al. "Survey of Winnipeg Restaurant Patrons' Attitudes toward Nonsmoking Areas." _Canadian Journal of Public Health_ 79, no. 4 (1988): 231-34.

496. Statistics Canada. Social Statistics Field. Special Surveys Group. _Crime / Victimization Survey Documentation: Canadian Urban Victimization Survey 1982: Interviewers Manual_. Programs Branch User Report, no. 1986-18. Ottawa, ON: Solicitor General Canada, 1986.

497. Stennett, R. G. "Semestering: Effects on Student Attitudes and Achievement: With Summaries in French, German and Spanish." _The Canadian Journal of Education_ 13, no. 4 (1988): 497-504.

498. Stevenson, H. Michael, and A. Paul Williams. "Physicians and Medicare: Professional Ideology and Canadian Health Care Policy." _Canadian Public Policy_ 11, no. 3 (1985): 504-21.

499. Storch, Janet L., and Herbert C. Northcott. "Hospital Administrators as Professionals: A Study of Occupational Role Identity." _Hospital & Health Services Administration_ 34, no. 4 (1989): 507-23.

500. Strain, Laurel A. "Illness Behavior in Old Age: From Symptom Awareness to Resolution." *Journal of Aging* 3, no. 4 (1989): 325-40.

501. Strain, Laurel A. "Physician Visits by the Elderly: Testing the Andersen-Newman Framework." *Canadian Journal of Sociology* 15, no. 1 (1990): 19-37.

502. Strain, Laurel A. "Use of Health Services in Later Life: The Influence of Health Beliefs." *Journal of Gerontology* 46, no. 3 (1991): S143-S150.

503. Sturgess, Pamela A. *An Exploration of the Character, Expressive Qualities and Attitudes towards Arts Activities of Exceptional Adolescent Students.* Toronto, ON: Ontario Ministry of Education, 1986.

504. Sussman, Susan. *Utilization of and Teachers' Attitudes toward Educational Television Facilities in the Schools of the Board of Education for the Borough of York.* Toronto, ON: Ontario Ministry of Education, Research and Evaluation Branch, Research Reports, 1973.

505. Svenson, Lawrence W., and Connie K. Varnhagen. "Knowledge, Attitudes and Behaviours Related to AIDS among First-Year University Students." *Canadian Journal of Public Health* 81, no. 2 (1990): 139-40.

506. Szawarski, Zbigniew et al. "Country Reports." *Hastings Center Report* 17, no. 3 (1987): S27- S36.

507. Tanner, Julian. "Reluctant Rebels: A Case Study of Edmonton High School Drop-Outs." *Canadian Review of Sociology and Anthropology* 27, no. 1 (1990): 74-94.

508. Tanner, Julian. "Youth Culture and the Canadian High School: An Empirical Analysis." *Canadian Journal of Sociology* 3, no. 1 (1978): 89-102.

509. Taylor, Alan Richard, and David F. Robitaille. *Classroom Processes and Their Relationship to Achievement in Mathematics: An Analysis of Factors Related to Students' Opinions about and Achievement in Mathematics.* Victoria, BC: British Columbia Ministry of Education, Student Assessment Branch, 1987.

510. Taylor, Malcolm et al. *Medical Perspectives on Canadian Medicare: Attitudes of Canadian Physicians to Policies and Problems of the Medical Care Insurance Program.* Downsview, ON: York University, Institute for Behavioural Research, 1984.

511. Tepperman, Lorne. "The Effect of Court Size on Organization and Procedure." *Canadian Review of Sociology and Anthropology* 10, no. 4 (1973): 346-65.

512. Thomas, E. M., and F. R. Wake. *Effects of Health Education on Smoking Habits in School Students - A Longitudinal Study - Part 1 - Smoking Behavior and Attitudes of Grade 7 Ottawa Students, Jan. 1969.* Ottawa, ON: Department of National Health and Welfare, 1972.

513. Tilly, Anthony, and Peter Myers. *The Influence of Wordprocessing on the Attitudes and Writing of Postsecondary Students.* Education and Technology Series. Toronto, ON: Ministry of Education, 1988.

514. Tinney, Mary-Anne. "Role Perceptions in Foster Parent Associations in British Columbia." *Child Welfare* 64, no. 1 (1985): 73-79.

515. Tolsma, Catherine Colette. *Relationships between Two Methods of Vocabulary Instruction, Vocabulary Achievement, Reading Attitude, and Locus of Control in a Community College Reading Course.* ERIBC Reports, no. 82:7. Vancouver, BC: Educational Research Institute of British Columbia, 1982.

516. Valeriote, Sherron O. "Marriage and Parenting: An Evaluation of the Impact of a Film-Discussion Group Program on Attitude." M.Sc. thesis, University of Guelph, 1987.

517. Valliant, Paul M. et al. "Mental Health in a Remote Community." *Psychological Reports* 53 (August 1983): 95-100.

518. Van Der Keilen, Marguerite. "Some Effects of a Special Indian Culture Oriented Program on Attitudes of White and Indian Elementary School Pupils." *Canadian Journal of Behavioural Science* 9, no. 2 (1977): 161-68.

519. Van der Merwe, Sandra. "Women as Managers: The Current Attitudes and Programs of Canadian Businessmen." *Business Quarterly* 44 (Spring 1979): 35-39.

520. Varnhagen, Connie K. "Sexually Transmitted Diseases and Condoms: High School Students' Knowledge, Attitudes and Behaviours." *Canadian Journal of Public Health* 82, no. 2 (1991): 129-32.

521. Violato, Claudio, and LeRoy D. Travis. "National Survey of Education Students: Some Data on Background, Habits, and Reasons for Entering Education." *The Canadian Journal of Education* 15, no. 3 (1990): 277-92.

522. Wahlstrom, M. W. *Analysis of Teacher Beliefs in Relation to Procedures for Assessing Student Achievement.* Toronto, ON: Ontario Ministry of Education, Research and Evaluation Branch, 1976.

523. Walker, Jan A. et al. "Parental Attitudes toward Pediatric Organ Donation: A Survey." *Canadian Medical Association Journal* 142, no. 12 (1990): 1383-87.

524. Wallace, Bruce. "Mood on Campus: Students Are Nervous and Uncertain." *Maclean's* 104, no. 42 (1991): 24-27.

525. Wargon, Sylvia T. "Household and Family in Canada: A General Review of Recent Demographic Trends." *International Journal of Sociology of the Family* 8, no. 1 (1978): 53-68.

526. Wasson, David K. *Community-Based Preventive Policing: A Review.* Programs Branch User Report, no. 1984-90. Ottawa, ON: Ministry of the Solicitor General, 1984.

527. Watts, Lyle Charles. "Changing Irrational Beliefs of Students: The Effect of Teachers." M.Ed. thesis, University of Alberta, 1972.

528. Waxler-Morrison, Nancy et al. *Cross-Cultural Caring: A Handbook for Health Professionals in Western Canada.* Vancouver, BC: Univeristy of British Columbia Press, 1990.

529. Weiss, Joel et al. *Balancing the Scales, Gender and Group Differences: Literacy and Interest in Science and Technology.* Toronto, ON: Ontario Institute for Studies in Education, 1994.

530. Wilkins, M. L. *Correctional Officers - Roles, Attitudes and Problems.* Toronto, ON: Ontario Ministry of Correctional Services, Planning and Research, 1975.

531. Williams, A. Paul et al. "Medicine and the Canadian State: From the Politics of Conflict to the Politics of Accomodation?" *Journal of Health & Social Behavior* 36, no. 4 (1995): 303-21.

532. Williams, A. Paul et al. "Women in Medicine: Practice Patterns and Attitudes." *Canadian Medical Association Journal* 143, no. 3 (1990): 194-201.

533. Williams, Tom R., and H. Millinoff. *Canada's Schools: Report Card for the 1990's: A CEA Opinion Poll.* Toronto, ON: Canadian Education Association, 1990.

534. Wilson, H. T. "Attitudes toward Science: Canadian and American Scientists." *International Journal of Comparative Sociology* 18, no. 1-2 (1977): 154-75.

535. Winzer, Margaret. *Teacher Attitudes toward the Mainstreaming of Exceptional Students: Effects of the Educational Climate.* Vancouver, BC: Educational Research Institute of British Columbia, 1986.

536. Yarmey, A. Daniel. "Accuracy and the Credibility of the Elderly Witness [The Relative Accuracy of Memory and Credibility of the Aged Witness to Give Testimony in Court; Their Attitudes toward Officers of the Court, Canada]." *Canadian Journal on Aging* 3 (1984): 79-90.

537. Yarmey, A. Daniel. "Attitudes and Sentencing for Sexual Assault as a Function of Age and Sex of Subjects." *Canadian Journal on Aging* 4 (1985): 20-28.

538. Zachariah, Mathew. "Continuity between School Curriculum and Vocation: Manual Labour's Ineffective Role." *International Review of Education* 34, no. 2 (1988): 207-23.

539. Zamble, Edward et al. *An Analysis of Coping Behaviour in Prison Inmates.* Programs Branch User Report, no. 1984-77. Ottawa, ON: Ministry of the Solicitor General, 1984.

540. Zamble, Edward, and Kerry Lee Kalm. "General and Specific Measures of Public Attitudes toward Sentencing." *The Canadian Journal of Behavioural Science* 22, no. 3 (1990): 327-37.

541. Zheng, W., and Balakrishnan T. R. "Attitudes towards Cohabitation and Marriage in Canada." *Journal of Comparative Family Studies* 23, no. 1 (1992): 1-12.

542. Ziegler, Suzanne. "School for Life: The Experience of Italian Immigrants in Canadian Schools." *Human-Organization* 39, no. 3 (1980): 263-67.

543. Ziegler, Suzanne, and Merrijoy Kelner. *Mothers' Preventive Beliefs and Practices: Some Ethnic Variations.* Child in the City Report, 12. Toronto, ON: University of Toronto, Centre for Urban and Community Studies, 1981.

544. Zingle, Harvey W., and Sharon C. Anderson. "Irrational Beliefs and Teacher Stress." *The Canadian Journal of Education* 15, no. 4 (1990): 445-49.

Section 3

Economy and Labour Relations

545. "20% of Affluent Francophones Say Starting a Business Is a High Priority: Financial Times/ Decima Poll." *Financial Times of Canada* 77, no. 17 (1988): 5.

546. "57% of Canadians Believe a National Sales Tax Would Be Unfair." *Financial Times of Canada* 77, no. 35 (1989): 5.

547. "Attitudes toward Equal Opportunity in Employment: The Case of One Canadian Government Department." *Business Quarterly* 48, no. 1 (1983): 87-93.

548. "Company's Honesty, Ethical Behavior Top Concern for Workers: Poll." *This Week in Business* 2, no. 33 (1989): 13.

549. "Entrepreneurs Speak Out (Arthur Andersen & Co. Survey of Small Business Attitudes)." *Alberta Business* 7, no. 3 (1990): 29, 29b-d.

550. "Free Trade Reconsidered: CEO Survey." *Canadian Business* 64, no. 1 (1991): 36-41.

551. "Hard at Work: They May Not Be Big Gamblers, but Toronto's Executives Have an Admirable Work Ethic." *Metropolitan Business Journal* 78, no. 1 (1988): 18-19.

552. "Japan and Canada: A Big Difference in Attitudes." *Manitoba Business* (May/June 1982): 70.

553. "Make Room for a Maverick (Executives of Major Corporations Give Their Views of Public Relations)." *Marketing* 94, no. 4 (1989): 11-12, 14.

554. "No Holds Barred: A Vote of Support for Free Trade and Sunday Shopping (Attitudes of Toronto Executives)." *Metropolitan Toronto Business Journal* 78, no. 1 (1988): 25.

555. "Rethinking Attitudes and Strategies." *Au Courant (Eng.)* 11, no. 2 (1990): 5-7.

556. "Share Ownership Up Strongly in Canada, TSE Survey Says (Canadian Shareholders: Their Profile and Attitudes)." *Northern Miner* 75, no. 43 (1990): 5.

557. "Welfare or Workfare: Some People Believe That Welfare Recipients Should be Forced to Work on Community Projects." *Canada and the World* 54, no. 7 (1989): 20-21.

558. Adcom Research Limited, and Canadian International Development Agency. Public Affairs Division. *Report on Canadians' Attitudes toward Foreign Aid, November 1980.* Hull, PQ: Canadian International Development Agency, 1981.

559. Alberta. Alberta Department of Career Development and Employment. *Survey of Calgary Employers Expectations of Job Applicants.* Calgary, AB: The Department, 1989.

560. Allen, Lynne (Lynne Veronica). *Survey of Student Attitudes on Entrepreneurship and Small Business.* Small Business Advocacy Report, no. 31. Toronto, ON: Ministry of Industry, Trade and Technology, Small Business, Service Industries and Capital Projects Division, 1989.

561. Anderson, John C. "Local Union Participation: A Re-Examination." *Industrial Relations* 18, no. 1 (1979): 18-31.

562. Angus Reid Group. *Future Trends in Housing.* Ottawa, ON: Canada Mortgage and Housing Corporation, 1995.

563. Atkinson, Tom. "Changing Attitudes toward Work in Canada: Differences between Male and Female Attitudes toward Work." *The Canadian Business Review* 10 (Summer 1983): 47-51.

564. Baer, Douglas E. et al. "Economic Dissatisfaction, Potential Unionism, and Attitudes toward Unions in Canada." *The Canadian Review of Sociology and Anthropology* 28, no. 1 (1991): 67-83.

565. Bajrak, Andrew, and Ken Sharratt. *Inter City Transportation - Public Attitudes and Perceived Social Impact Associated with Upgrading Inner City Transportation in Eastern Ontario.* Toronto, ON: Ministry of Transportation and Communications, Research and Development Division, 1976.

566. Baker, Patricia. "Doing Fieldwork in a Canadian Bank: Issues of Gender and Power." *Resources for Feminist Research* 16, no. 4 (1987): 45-47.

567. Barber, Clarence L. *Manitoba's Interest in and Attitude towards a Proposed Canada United States Free Trade Area - Discussion Papers on Free Trade*. Winnipeg, MB: Manitoba Department of Industry, Trade and Technology, 1985.

568. Bassler, J. F., K. R. MacCrimmon, and W. T. Starbury. *Risk Attitudes of U. S. and Canadian Top Managers*. Research Reports, 5. Ottawa, ON: Industry, Trade and Commerce, Technology Branch, 1973.

569. Bata, Sonja. "Nurturing a Global Attitude." *Canadian Business Review* 18, no. 3 (1991): 35-37.

570. Benedict, D. *Working Participation in Decision Making in Industry: Forms, Experiences and Attitudes*. Hamilton, ON: McMaster University, Labour Studies Programme, 1978.

571. Borg, Vince. "Health in the Workplace: Our Attitudes Are Hardening." *Financial Times of Canada* 76, no. 36 (1988): 3.

572. British Columbia. Legislative Assembly. Select Standing Committee on Agriculture. *British Columbia Food Shoppers Attitudes and Behaviour - Phase 3 Research Report*. Victoria, BC: The Committee, 1978.

573. Brown, Judith K., and Jack Quarter. "Resistance to Change: The Influence of Social Networks on the Conversion of a Privately Owned Unionized Business to a Worker Cooperative." *Economic and Industrial Democracy* 15, no. 2 (1994): 259-82.

574. Bryant, Robyn. "Uneasiness Permeates Anglophone Business Community." *This Week in Business* 3, no. 1 (1990): 1, 3.

575. Cachon, Jean Charles. *Venture Creators and Firm Buyers: A Comparison of Attitudes towards Government Help and Locus of Control*. Wellesley, MA: Center for Entrepreneurial Studies, Babson College, Georgia Institute of Technology, College of Management, 1988.

576. Canada. Department of Communications. *Survey of Public Attitudes towards the Computer*. Ottawa, ON: Information Canada, 1973.

577. Canada. Department of External Affairs. *Report to the Department of External Affairs on Attitudes toward Canada-U.S. Free Trade, October 1987*. Ottawa, ON: The Department, 1987.

578. Canada. Employment and Immigration Advisory Council. *Workers with Family Responsibilities in a Changing Society: Who Cares?; Who Cares: Workers with Family Responsibilities in a Changing Society*. Ottawa, ON: The Council, 1987.

579. Canada. Ministry of Consumer and Commercial Relations, and Market Facts of Canada Limited. *Study of Attitudes in Ontario*. Toronto, ON: Ministry of Consumer and Commercial Relations, 1979.

580. Canada. Post Office Department, and R. D. Vanderberg. *Post Office and Its Workers; Appraisal of Attitudes That Are Destroying a Vital Public Service*. Ottawa, ON: Carleton University, Department of Economics, [1971].

581. Canadian Centre for Occupational Health and Safety, and Joint Federal-Provincial Inquiry Commission into Safety in Mines and Mining Plants in Ontario (Canada). *Review of the Literature on Attitudes and Roles and Their Effects on Safety in the Workplace*. Hamilton, ON: Canadian Centre for Occupational Health and Safety, 1980.

582. Canadian Inter-mark. *Research Survey on Attitudes and Uses by Riders and Non-Riders of the Toronto Transit Commission*. Toronto, ON: Canadian Inter-mark, 1976.

583. Canadian Labour Congress. *Submission to the Legislative Committee on Bill C-45: The Parliamentary Employment and Staff Relations Act*. Ottawa, ON: The Congress, 1986.

584. Canadian Labour Market and Productivity Centre. Study Group on Technicians and Technologists. *Tapping Our Potential: Technicians and Technologists of Tomorrow*. Ottawa, ON: Canadian Labour Market and Productivity Centre, 1993.

585. Carmichael, Edward A., and Katie Macmillan. *Focus on Follow-Through: Policy Review and Outlook, 1988*. Toronto, ON: C. D. Howe Institute, 1988.

586. Caron, Normand. *Experiences, Attitudes and Intentions of the Québec Labour Movement with Respect to Paid Educational Leave*. Canada, Skill Development Leave Task Force, Background Paper, 20. Hull, PQ: Employment and Immigration Canada, 1983.

587. Carter, Peter. "Toronto Executive Survey: An Exclusive Look at How Metro's Business Leaders Feel." *Metropolitan Toronto Business Journal* 79, no. 2 (1989): 29-31, 33-36.

588. Chaison, Gary N., and P. Andiappan. "Profiles of Local Union Offices: Females vs. Males." *Industrial Relations* 26, no. 3 (1987): 281-83.

589. Chekki, Danesh A. *Citizen Attitudes toward City Services and Taxes.* Winnipeg, MB: University of Winnipeg, Institute of Urban Studies, 1985.

590. Clark, S. *Work, Work, Work: Impacts of Office Automation on Work, Workers, and Workplaces: Executive Summary.* Laval, PQ: Communications Canada, Canadian Workplace Automation Research Centre, Organizational Research Directorate, 1988.

591. Clayton Research Associates, and Canada Mortgage and Housing Corporation. *Lender Attitudes to Graduated Payment Mortgages and Social Housing Loans.* Ottawa, ON: Canada Mortgage and Housing Corporation, 1980.

592. Coburn, David. "Job-Worker Incongruence: Consequences for Health." *Journal of Health & Social Behavior* 16, no. 2 (1975): 198-212.

593. Cohen, Stanley A., and Anthony N. Doob. "Public Attitudes to Plea Bargaining." *Criminal Law Quarterly* 3, no. 1 (1989): 85-109.

594. Cole, C. W. "Breaking New Investment Ground [Changing Investment Operations and Attitudes of Banks in Canada]." *Canadian Banker* 84 (1977): 60+.

595. Conference Board of Canada. "Business Attitude Survey Reveals More Cheerful Economic Outlook." *Modern Purchasing* 25, no. 9 (1983): 4.

596. Conference Board of Canada. "Conference Board of Canada Survey: Business Attitudes Improving." *Sporting Goods Canada* 11, no. 7 (1983): 56-57.

597. Dana, Leo-Paul, and Kevin Hashem. "Coping in Cape Breton: Some Concrete Suggestions for Action -- The Most Important of Which Is a Change of Attitude." *Policy Options* 11, no. 4 (1990): 35.

598. Dangor, Joe, and Nathan Rudyk. "Is Your Overachiever an Imposter?" *Small Business* 9, no. 5 (1990): 64.

599. De Boer, Connie. "The Polls: Attitudes toward Work." *Public Opinion Quarterly* 42, no. 3 (1978): 414-23.

600. Decision Marketing Research Limited, and Ontario Small Business Branch. *Hours of Work and Overtime in Small Business*. Small Business Advocacy Report, no. 24. Toronto, ON: Ministry of Industry, Trade and Technology, Service Industries and Capital Projects Division, Small Business Branch, Small Business, 1988.

601. Deschenes, Lucie. *Computers in Daily Life: Canadians' Behaviour and Attitudes regarding Computer Technology*. Laval, PQ: Communications Canada, Canadian Workplace Automation Research Centre (CWARC), Organizational Research Directorate, 1988.

602. Deslauriers, Brian E., and Judy Zon. *Survey of Informational, Advertising and Promotional Activities of Ontario Transit Systems and Attitudes of Transit Officials*. Toronto, ON: Ministry of Transportation and Communications, Research and Development Division, 1977.

603. DeSorter, Harry. "Comments on: Causes and Intervention in Canadian Agriculture; Policy Processes in the Canadian Agricultural-Agribusiness Sector: Review Article." *The Canadian Journal of Agricultural Economics* 38, no. 4 (1990): 797-99.

604. Dhawan, K. C., and Ursula Tokateloff. *Attitudes toward Ethics: A Survey of Canadian Top Business Executives*. Montreal, PQ: Concordia University (Sir George William Campus), 1975.

605. Dugan, Ann. "Quebec Banks on Economic Power." *Economy: The Journal of the World's Capital and Money Markets* (1990): 74-76+.

606. Fitzgerald, John, and Janis Gershman. *Managerial Attitudes towards Part-Time Employment - A Study of Supervisory Personnel at the Toronto Board of Education*. Toronto Board of Education, Research Department, Research Service, 146. Toronto, ON: Board of Education, 1977.

607. Fletcher, Frederick J. *Canadian Attitudes toward Competitiveness and Entrepreneurship: A Report*. Ottawa, ON: Industry, Science and Technology Canada, 1992.

608. Frank, James G. "Recruiting in a Changing Environment: As More and Better Qualified Women Enter the Labour Force There Will Have to Be a Change in Attitudes among Employers." *Canadian Business Review* 8 (1981): 37-40.

609. Froese, Jane. "Warmer Reception." *Metropolitan Toronto Business Journal* 79, no. 4 (1989): 7.

610. Galbraith, J. William, and Conference Board of Canada. *Research and Development in the Canadian Corporate Sector, 1987: A Survey of Attitudes and Spending Intentions*. Ottawa, ON: Conference Board of Canada, 1987.

611. Gallagher, J. E. "Consumer Attitudes toward Children's Flame-Retardant Sleepwear." Ph.D. diss., University of Guelph, 1978.

612. Gardiner, W. L. *Public Acceptance of the New Information Technologies: The Role of Attitudes*. University of Montreal Gamma Information Society Project Paper, No. 1.9. Montreal, PQ: University of Montreal, Gamma Information Society Project; McGill University, Information Society Project, 1980.

613. Gartrell, John W., and N. M. Mendenhall. *Attitudes towards Changes in Communication Technology: The Introduction of Teleconferencing*. Ottawa, ON: Department of Communications, Communications Research Centre, 1975.

614. Goldfarb Consultants Limited, and Canada. Employment and Immigration Canada. *An Evaluation of Canadian Employers' Attitudes towards Unemployment Insurance, Canada Employment Centres, and Immigration*. Technical Study (Task Force on Unemployment Insurance) no. 4; Technical Study (Task Force on Labour Market Development), no. 37. Ottawa, ON: Employment and Immigration Canada, 1981.

615. Goldfarb Consultants Limited, and Vickers and Benson Limited. *The Female Culture: General Purchase Behaviour and Attitudes Section: A Research Report for Vickers & Benson Limited*. Canada: Goldfarb Consultants, 1976.

616. Grayson, J. Paul. "Political Consequences of Unemployment: An Application of the Power Model of Blue-Collar Radicalism." *Industrial Relations* 44, no. 3 (1989): 635-53.

617. Greeno, Daniel W., and George H. Haines. *Predicting Product Choice Behavior from Attitudes*. Working Paper, no. 8. Toronto, ON: University of Toronto/York University Joint Program in Transportation, 1977.

618. Grey, Ronald J., and Gail Cook Johnson. "Trends in Employee Attitudes: Differences between Canadian and American Workers." *Canadian Business Review* 15, no. 4 (1988): 24-27.

619. Hammond, A. E. "Consumer Knowledge of Selected Consumer Protection Laws and Related Attitudes, Complaint Behavior and Demographic." M.Sc. thesis, University of Guelph, 1979.

620. Herzog, J. P., and Human Rights Commission of British Columbia. *Mandatory Retirement in British Columbia: A Review of Issues, Practices, and Attitudes.* Victoria, BC: The Commission, 1980.

621. Hurl, Lorna F. "Privatization of Social Services: Time to Move the Debate Along." *Canadian Public Policy* 12, no. 3 (1986): 507-12.

622. Insight Canada Research. "Toronto Executive Survey." *Metropolitan Toronto Business Journal* 78, no. 1 (1988): 17-25.

623. International Communications Agency. *Canadian Attitudes toward the U.S. Economic and Cultural Presence in Canada.* Research Report, R-35-78. Washington, DC: The Agency, 1978.

624. Johnson, Gail Cook, and Ronald J. Grey. "Trends in Employee Attitudes: Employee Motivation in High-Performance Companies." *Canadian Business Review* 15, no. 3 (1988): 26-29.

625. Johnson, Gail Cook, and Ronald J. Grey. "Trends in Employee Attitudes: Signs of Diminishing Employee Commitment." *Canadian Business Review* 15, no. 1 (1988): 20-23.

626. Johnson, Laura Climenko. *Youth and Employment: Baseline Report on Young People's Work Experience and Attitudes.* Toronto, ON: Joint Task Force on Youth and Employment and Social Planning Council of Metro Toronto, 1986.

627. Johnston, William Atchison. "Class and Economic Nationalism: Attitudes toward Foreign Investment." *Canadian Journal of Sociology* 10, no. 1 (1985): 23-36.

628. Kalin, Rudolf, and Donald S. Rayko. "Discrimination in Evaluative Judgments against Foreign Accented Job Candidates." *Psychological Reports* 43, no. 3 (2) (1978): 1203-09.

629. Kallen, Evelyn, and Merrijoy Kelner. *Ethnicity, Opportunity and Successful Entrepreneurship in Canada.* Downsview, ON: York University, Institute for Behavioural Research, Ethnic Research Programme, 1983.

630. Kates, Peat Marwick & Co. *Foreign Ownership - Corporate Behaviour and Public Attitudes: Overview Report.* Toronto, ON: Select Committee on Economic and Cultural Nationalism of the Legislative Assembly of Ontario, 1974.

politan Toronto, (Ont.). Transportation Division. *Scarborough own Centre Light Rail Transit: Survey of Community Attitudes, eport 3.* Toronto, ON: Metropolitan Toronto Planning epartment, 1975.

Katherine. "The Influence of Gender on Work Activities and titudes of Senior Civil Servants in the United States, Canada, d Great Britain." *Research in Politics and Society* 2 (1986): 3-99.

y, Jean. "Management Survey: What Canada's Chief Executives e Thinking." *The Financial Post* 83, no. 46 (1989): 63-65.

, J. Alex, and Lawrence Leduc. *Cross-Sectional Analysis of nadian Public Attitudes toward U.S. Equity Investment in nada.* Working Paper Series, 2/75. Toronto, ON: Ontario onomic Council, 1975.

, Michael A., and Tom Atkinson. "Gender Differences in rrelates of Job Satisfaction." *Canadian Journal of Behavioural ience* 13, no. 1 (1981): 44-52.

ski, Leon, and David A. Wolfe. "New Technology and Training: ssons from Abroad." *Canadian Public Policy* 15, no. 3 (1989): 5-64.

u, C. T. "Attitude of Government and Industry toward the nsumers' Association of Canada." M.Sc. thesis, University of elph, 1972.

Kelly. "Building in Quality: The Actions of Senior Executives st Demonstrate Their Commitment." *Canadian Business view* 18, no. 4 (1991): 22-25.

D. et al. "Attitudes towards Foreign Products and International ce Competition." *The Canadian Journal of Economics* 24, no. 1 91): 1-11.

gale, Donald V., and Jean-Marie Toulouse. "Values, Structure, cess, and Reactions/Adjustments: A Comparison of French and glish Canadian Industrial Organizations." *Canadian Journal of avioural Science* 9, no. 1 (1977): 37-48.

Legislative Assembly. Select Committee on Economic and tural Nationalism, and Kates, Peat, Marwick & Co. *Overview ort; Part of a Study on Foreign Ownership: Corporate aviour and Public Attitudes.* [Toronto], ON: The Committee, 1.

631. Keenleyside, Terrence A., Lawrence LeDuc, and J. Alex Murray. "Public Opinion and Canada-United States Economic Relations." *Behind the Headlines* 35, no. 4 (1976).

632. Kehoe, Mary. "Job-Entry Discrimination: Survey of Toronto Employers." *Canadian Labour* 30 (1985): 12-15.

633. Kelly, Maria V. *The Relationship between Employment Status and Attitudes regarding Work.* Toronto, ON: Ontario Ministry of Correctional Services, 1981.

634. Kingston, Anne. "Attitudes to Debt Need as Much Overhaul as the Bankruptcy Act." *Financial Times of Canada* 79, no. 52 (1991): 15.

635. Knoop, Robert, and Alexander Sanders. *Furniture Industry: Attitudes towards Exporting.* Technological Innovation Studies Program, Research Report, 44. Ottawa, ON: Industry, Trade and Commerce, Technology Branch, 1978.

636. Krahn, Harvey et al. "Explanations of Unemployment in Canada." *International Journal of Comparative Sociology* 28, no. 3-4 (1987): 228-36.

637. Krahn, Harvey, and Trevor Harrison. "'Self-referenced' Relative Deprivation and Economic Beliefs: The Effects of the Recession in Alberta." *Canadian Review of Sociology and Anthropology* 29, no. 2 (1992): 191-209.

638. Krahn, Harvey, and Graham S. Lowe. "Public Attitudes towards Unions: Some Canadian Evidence." *Journal of Labor Research* 5, no. 2 (1984): 149-64.

639. La Palombara, Joseph, and Stephen Blank. *Multinational Corporations and National Elites: A Study in Tensions.* Conference Board Report, no. 702. New York, NY: Conference Board, 1976.

640. Langford, Tom. "Involvement with Unions, Union Belief Perspectives, and Desires for Union Membership." *Journal of Labor Research* 15, no. 3 (1994): 257-70.

641. Langford, Tom. "Workers' Subordinate Values: A Canadian Case Study." *Canadian Journal of Sociology* 11, no. 3 (1986): 269-91.

642. Lanphier, M. et al. *Analysis of Attitudes toward Unemployment Insurance.* Research Report, ANA. North York, ON: York University, Institute for Behavioural Research, 1970.

643. Larter, Sylvia et al. *Students' Attitudes to Work and Unemployment: Part 2 - The Attitude Questionnaire*. Toronto, ON: Board of Education for the City of Toronto, Research Department, 1978.

644. Larter, Sylvia, and John Fitzgerald. *Students' Attitudes to Work and Unemployment: Pt. 3 - The Open-Ended and True-False Questions*. Toronto, ON: Board of Education for the City of Toronto, Research Department, 1978.

645. LeBrasseur, Roland. "Retirement and Skill Issues in Northern Ontario Industries." *Industrial Relations* 45, no. 2 (1990): 268-80.

646. Leman, Marc. *Canadian-American Relations: Significant Developments*. Current Issue Review, 79-34E. Ottawa, ON: Library of Parliament, Research Branch, 1987.

647. Leroux, P. "Study of Employee Participation and Attitudes of the Recreation Program at the Mutual Life Assurance Company of Canada, Head Office, Waterloo." Master's thesis, University of Waterloo, Department of Recreation, 1978.

648. Lightman, Ernie S. "Economics of Supply of Canada's Military Manpower." *Industrial Relations* 14, no. 2 (1975): 209-19.

649. Lipsey, Richard G., and Murray G. Smith. *Global Imbalances and U.S. Policy Responses: A Canadian Perspective*. Toronto, ON: C. D. Howe Institute; Washington, DC: National Planning Association, 1987.

650. Livingstone, D. W., and Meg Luxton. "Gender Consciousness at Work: Modification of the Male Breadwinner Norm among Steelworkers and Their Spouses." *Canadian Review of Sociology and Anthropology* 26, no. 2 (1989): 240-75.

651. London, Ontario. Committee for International Development. *Report of a Survey of Attitudes of the Citizens of London, Ontario towards International Development*. London, ON: The Committee, 1970.

652. Long, Richard J. "Worker Ownership and Job Attitudes: A Field Study." *Industrial Relations* 21, no. 2 (1982): 196-215.

653. Lowe, Graham S., and Harvey Krahn. "Recent Trends in Public Support for Unions in Canada." *Journal of Labor Research* 10, no. 4 (1989): 391-410.

654. Lowe, Graham S., and Harvey Krahn. "Where Wives Work: The Relative Effects of Situational and Attitudinal Factors." *Canadian Journal of Sociology* 10, no. 1 (1985): 1-22.

655. Luce, Sally R., and Gene R. Swimmer and Safety in Three Asbestos Bre Series, no. 6. Toronto, ON: Royal and Safety Arising from the Use

656. MacCrimmon, Kenneth R., and Dona Risk Measures." *Theory and Dec*

657. Macmillan, Katie. *Women and Free T* Toronto, ON: C. D. Howe Institu

658. Mallen, Bruce E., and Jean Francois *Attitudes of Canadian Freight a* Montreal, PQ: Sir George Willia

659. Marshall Fenn Ltd. *Study of Attitud Relating to the Apprenticeship S* Ministry of Education, 1976.

660. Marton, Katherin. "Attitudes toward Study of the Canadian Blue Col Canada." Ph.D. diss., New York Business Administration, 1973.

661. Marzolini, Michael, and Peter Carte Towers: Executive Survey." *Me Journal* 80, no. 6 (1990): 27-32.

662. McInnes, David. "And Now - - Cons Having a Bigger Impact on Ho *Magazine* 23, no. 12 (1989): 36-

663. McKie, Craig. "American Managers *International Journal of Comp* 44-62.

664. McLaren, K. Louise. "Accommodati *Canadian Banker* 97, no. 6 (19

665. McNeil, Jeannine, and Micheline G *Processing and Automated Dat and Quality of Users' Jobs: Su* Workplace Automation Resear Directorate, 1989.

666. McShane, Steven L. "General Unio *Journal of Labor Research* 7, n

667. Metro

668. Meye

669. Murp

670. Murra

671. Murra

672. Muszy

673. Nakat

674. Nelson

675. Never,

676. Nighti

677. Ontari

678. Ontario. Ministry of Transportation and Communications. *Communications in Ontario - Findings of a Survey of Public Attitudes*. Toronto, ON: The Ministry, 1973.

679. Papadopoulos, Nicolas et al. "An International Comparative Analysis of Consumer Attitudes toward Canada and Canadian Products." *Canadian Journal of Administrative Sciences* 11, no. 3 (1994): 224-39.

680. Pasnak, William. "New Corporate Attitude." *The Canadian* 3, no. 9 (1990): 16-18.

681. Peitchinis, Stephen G. *Attitude of Trade Unions towards Technological Changes*. Canada Department of Industry, Trade and Commerce, Office of Science and Technology, Research Report. Ottawa, ON: Industry, Trade and Commerce, Technology Branch, 1980.

682. Pinfield, Lawrence T., and Mark N. Wexler. "Pre-Employment Work Values of Canadian High School Students." *Free Inquiry in Creative Sociology* 10, no. 2 (1982): 231-36.

683. Poirer, Mark, and Bonnie Boyd. *1979 Merchants' Survey: The Results and Analysis of Results from a Questionnaire Survey Sampling the Attitudes of Downtown Merchants toward Their Own Business and the Downtown in General, Carried Out in the Summer of 1979*. Halifax, NS: Department of Municipal Affairs, Community Planning Division, 1979.

684. Ponak, Allen. "Faculty Collective Bargaining: A Cross-Cultural Survey." *Journal of Collective Negotiations in the Public Sector* 16, no. 3 (1987): 219-32.

685. Ponak, Allen, and Tom Janz. "A Comparison of Public and Private Sector Union Attitudes in Canada." *Journal of Collective Negotiations in the Public Sector* 13, no. 3 (1984): 211-23.

686. Potvin, Jean. "Tax Evasion in Canada." *Canadian Tax Journal* 25 (May/June 1977): 229-45.

687. Rayruse, Bruce. *The Leading Indicator Properties of Surveyed Consumer Attitudes and Buying Intentions*. Technical Report, 30. Ottawa, ON: Bank of Canada, 1982.

688. Rinehart, James W. "Contradictions of Work-Related Attitudes and Behaviour: An Interpretation." *Canadian Review of Sociology and Anthropology* 15, no. 1 (1978): 1-15.

689. Robb, R. E., and M. Gunderson. *Women and Overtime*. Toronto, ON: Ontario Task Force on Hours of Work and Overtime, 1987.

690. Robertson, Gordon, and P. Ferlejowski. *Employee Attitudes toward Compressed Work Schedules in Ontario: A Case Study of Ten Firms*. Employment Information Series, 6. Toronto, ON: Ontario Ministry of Labour, Research Branch, 1974.

691. Rogers, Judy. *Attitudes towards Alternative Work Arrangements - A Qualitative Assessment among Employers in Metropolitan Toronto*. Toronto, ON: Social Planning Council of Metropolitan Toronto, 1986.

692. Rosenfeld, Rachel A. "A Cross National Comparison of the Gender Gap in Income." *American Journal of Sociology* 96, no. 1 (1990): 69-106.

693. Ryant, Joseph C., and Canada. Department of Regional Economic Expansion. Social and Human Analysis Branch. *Work Organizations, Behaviour and Attitudes*. Ottawa, ON: Department of Regional Economic Expansion, Social and Human Analysis Branch, 1970.

694. Saporta, Ishak, and Bryan Lincoln. "Managers' and Workers' Attitudes toward Unions in the U.S. and Canada." *Industrial Relations* 50, no. 3 (1995): 550-66.

695. Schachter, Harvey. "Power Shift." *Canadian Business* 68 (August 1995): 20-28.

696. Schom-Moffat, Patti. "Whose Problem Is It? . . . Employees' Attitude towards Customer Service." *BC Business* 18, no. 11 (1990): 58-61.

697. Smith, Charlie. "Dateline Cloud Nine: Economy '90." *Equity Magazine* 7, no. 10 (1990): 16-17, 19+.

698. Smith, Geoffrey C. "Elderly Consumer Cognitions of Urban Shopping Centres." *Canadian Geographer* 33, no. 4 (1989): 353-59.

699. Smith, Michael R. "The Effects of Strikes on Workers: A Critical Analysis." *Canadian Journal of Sociology* 3, no. 4 (1978): 457-72.

700. Steed, Guy et al. *A National Consultation on Emerging Technology*. Discussion Paper. Ottawa, ON: Science Council of Canada, 1986.

701. Stickel, C. M. "Consumer Attitudes toward Canadian-Made Apparel Products." M.Sc. thesis, University of Guelph, 1980.

702. Swidinsky, Robert. "Working Wives, Income Distribution and Poverty." *Canadian Public Policy* 9, no. 1 (1983): 71-80.

703. Sztaba, Teresa L., and Nina Lee Colwill. "Secretarial and Management Students: Attitudes, Attributes, and Career Choice Considerations." *Sex Roles* 19 (1988): 651-65.

704. Tanner, Julian. "Skill Levels of Manual Workers and Beliefs about Work, Management, and Industry: A Comparison of Craft and Non-Craft Workers in Edmonton." *Canadian Journal of Sociology* 9, no. 3 (1984): 303-18.

705. Taylor, Donald M. "Anglophone and Francophone Managers' Perceptions of Cultural Differences in Approaches to Work." *Canadian Journal of Behavioural Science* 14, no. 2 (1982): 144-51.

706. Tmej, Luisa. *Consumer Attitudes Concerning Direct Farm Sales Outlets, Ontario, 1988*. Economics Information, no. 89-07. Toronto, ON: Ontario Ministry of Agriculture and Food, Economics and Policy Coordination Branch, 1989.

707. Toronto Stock Exchange. *Canadian Shareowners: Their Profile and Attitudes*. Toronto, ON: Toronto Stock Exchange, 1984.

708. Tougas, Francine et al. "Men's Attitudes toward Affirmative Action: Justice and Intergroup Relations at the Crossroads." *Social Justice Research* 8, no. 1 (1995): 57-71.

709. Townson, Monica. *Women's Labour Force Participation, Fertility Rates, and the Implications for Economic Development and Government Policy*. Discussion Paper on the Demographic Review, 87.A.11. Ottawa, ON: Institute for Research on Public Policy, Studies in Social Policy, 1987.

710. Wall, Marjorie, and L. A. Heslop. *Consumer Attitudes toward Canadian versus Foreign-Made Apparel*. Guelph, ON: University of Guelph, Department of Consumer Studies, 1985.

711. Waterloo Region Review Commission. *Public Attitude Survey*. Waterloo, ON: The Commission, 1978.

712. Wetzel, Kurt et al. "Union Commitment among Cooperative and Private Sector Retail Workers." *Annals of Public and Cooperative Economics* 63, no. 1 (1992): 55-75.

713. Williamson, D. R., and John W. Gartrell. *Employee Work Attitudes and Work Behaviour in Canadian Business*. Discussion Paper, no. s1. Ottawa, ON: Economic Council of Canada, 1976.

714. Winter, Steve. "Shopping Attitudes." *Canadian Moneysaver* 7, no. 5
        (1988): 133.

715. Woiceshyn, Janna. "Technological Leaders, Followers and Managerial
        Work Processes." *International Journal of Sociology and Social
        Policy* 9, no. 5-6 (1989): 39-56.

716. Wyckham, R. *Attitudes toward Spending, Saving and Borrowing: An
        Exploratory Study*. Discussion Paper Series, 74-06-01. Burnaby,
        BC: Simon Fraser University, Department of Economics and
        Commerce, 1974.

717. Yokom, John. "Gut-Meter Challenge Unveiled (Canadian and American
        Attitudes on the Effectiveness of Sales Promotion)." *Marketing* 95,
        no. 32 (1990): 12.

718. Young, Richard Anthony. "Career Development: Values, Attitudes, and
        Behavior in Rural Adolescent Males." Ph.D. diss., McGill
        University, 1977.

Section 4

Environment

719. Baseline Market Research. *Survey of Public Attitudes towards Energy Conservation: Research Recommendations*. Fredericton, NB: Department of Natural Resources and Energy, Mines and Resources, 1988.

720. Bates, Sheena. *The DIAND Socio-Economic Impact Monitoring Program: Attitudes towards the Normal Wells Project*. DIAND Monitoring Reports, no. 2-84. Ottawa, ON: Indian and Northern Affairs Canada, Northern Affairs Program, 1984.

721. BC Hydro, and Goldfarb Consultants Limited. *Public Attitudes toward BC Hydro: A Research Report*. Vancouver, BC: BC Hydro, 1988.

722. Beak Associates Consulting. *Local Concerns Assessment of Three Potential Reservoir Sites in the Little Bow River Basin*. Edmonton, AB: Alberta Environment, Planning Division, 1986.

723. Bergstrom, Eunice D. *Farmer-Wildlife Survey: Attitudes of Farmers toward Wildlife, Wildlife Use, and Habitat Retention in Saskatchewan*. Wildlife Technical Report, 85-3. Saskatoon, SK: Saskatchewan Parks and Renewable Resources, 1985.

724. Berris, C., and P. Bekker. *Logging in Kootenay Landscapes: The Public Response*. Land Management Report, no. 57. Victoria, BC: British Columbia Ministry of Forests and Lands, 1989.

725. Brightwell, Harry. *Parliamentary Forum on Global Climate Change*. Ottawa, ON: Queen's Printer, 1992.

726. Canada. Department of Energy, Mines and Resources. *Study of the Canadian Public's Attitudes toward Specific Energy Issues Facing Canadians - Supplement to Wave IV*. Montreal, PQ: Montreal Centre de Recherches Contemporaines, 1978.

727. Canada. Department of Transport. *Survey of Attitudes in Communities Adjacent to Vancouver International Airport*. Vancouver, BC.: Transport Canada, 1978.

728. Canada. Inland Waters Directorate, and J. Elizabeth McMeiken. *Public Health Professionals and the Environment: Study of Perception and Attitudes*. Social Science Series, 5. Ottawa, ON: Canada Inland Waters Directorate, 1972.

729. Canadian Environmental Advisory Council, and World Commission on Environment and Development. *Canada and Sustainable Development: A Commentary on Our Common Future: The Report of the World Commission on Environment and Development and Its Implications for Canada*. Ottawa, ON: Canadian Environmental Advisory Council, 1987.

730. Canadian Facts Company: Wave. *A Survey of the Public's Attitudes toward the Energy Situation, 1979*. Toronto, ON: Energy Mines and Resources Canada, 1979.

731. Canadian Gallup Poll Limited, and Canadian Forestry Service. *A Survey of the Public's Perceptions of, and Attitudes to the Forestry Industry in Canada*. Toronto, ON: Canadian Gallup Poll, 1986.

732. Canadian Waste Management Conference. *Wastetech '91, Canadian Waste Management Conference: Proceedings*. Hull, PQ: Environment Canada, Environmental Protection, 1991.

733. Canadian Wildlife Service. *The Importance of Wildlife to Canadians: Highlights of the 1991 Survey*. Ottawa, ON: Environment Canada, Canadian Wildlife Service, 1993.

734. Carlisle, Alan, and L. Chatarpaul. *Intensive Forestry: Some Socio-Economic and Environmental Concerns*. Information Report, PI-X-43. Chalk River, ON: Agriculture Canada, Canadian Forestry Service, Petawawa National Forestry Institute, 1984.

735. Compusave Inc., and Canada. Consumer and Corporate Affairs Canada. *Attitude Study on Gaseous Fuels*. Ottawa, ON: Consumer and Corporate Affairs Canada, 1983.

736. Connoly, S. J. (Stephen John). "Beliefs and Attitudes regarding Conservation Tillage." M.Sc. thesis, University of Guelph, 1988.

737. Contemporary Research Centre. *Study of the Canadian Public's Attitudes towards the Energy Situation in Canada. A Quantitative Trend Study Conducted in Selected Major Urban Centres in Canada, of the Attitudes of Both Men and Women toward the Subject of Energy*. Ottawa, ON: Energy, Mines and Resources Canada, 1978.

738. Davies, J. E. O., and J. K. Dobson. *Canadian Attitudes to Nuclear Power*. AECL, 5714. Chalk River, ON: Chalk River Nuclear Laboratories, 1975.

739. De Boer, Connie, and Ineke Catsburg. "The Impact of Nuclear Accidents on Attitudes toward Nuclear Energy." *Public Opinion Quarterly* 52, no. 2 (1988): 254-61.

740. Decima Research Ltd., and Canada. Environment Canada. *Canadians and the Environment: Attitudes and Choices*. Ottawa, ON: Decima Research, 1990.

741. Delude, Camille. *Opinions and Attitudes of Canadians Concerning Environment Quality*. Ottawa, ON: Environment Canada, 1978.

742. DeSantis, Solange. "How CEOs See Top Environment Issues." *The Financial Post* 83, no. 47 (1989): 23.

743. Donaldson, Sven. "About Attitude Adjustment (regarding Environmental Issues)." *Pacific Yachting* 33, no. 6 (1991): 44.

744. Eagles, Paul F. J. "Community Values and the Protection of Environmentally Sensitive Areas." *Society and Leisure* 8, no. 1 (1985): 205-16.

745. Environics Research Group. *1989 National Survey of Canadian Public Opinion on Forestry Issues*. Ottawa, ON: Forestry Canada, 1989.

746. Federal-Provincial Task Force for the 1987 National Survey on the Importance of Wildlife to Canadians. *The Importance of Wildlife to Canadians in 1987: Highlights of a National Survey*. Ottawa, ON: Environment Canada, Canadian Wildlife Service, 1989.

747. Flockton, P. R. *Municipal Solid Waste; Origins, Attitudes, and Management*. N.p., 1971.

748. Free, Brian Michael. *A Social Perspective of Recycling in Alberta*. Edmonton, AB: Environment Council of Alberta, 1986.

749. Gelber, Arthur E. "Culture, Cake and the Environment: Canadian Attitudes toward the Environment Reflect Cultural Immaturity." *Alternatives* 17, no. 4 (1991): 18-21.

750. Greer-Wooten, Bryn, and Lance Mitson. *Nuclear Power and the Canadian Public: A National and Regional Assessment of Public Attitudes and Perceptions of the Use of Nuclear Power for the Production of Electricity*. Research Report. Toronto, ON: York University, Institute for Behavioural Research, 1976.

751. Hansen, John Anthony Gervase. *Attitudes to Land Use and Planning: A Survey of Puslinch Township.* Reportings. Guelph, ON: University of Guelph, School of Rural Planning and Development, 1988.

752. Hewings, John Meredith. "Environmental Indices and Public Attitudes: The Case of the Ontario Air Pollution Index." Ph.D. diss., University of Toronto, 1975.

753. Ian Fenwick & Associates Inc., and Canada. Consumer and Corporate Affairs. *Profile of Oil-Using Households in Ontario.* Ottawa, ON: Consumer and Corporate Affairs Canada, 1984.

754. Jackson, Edgar Lionel. "Environmental Attitudes and Recreation Behaviour of Residents in Edmonton, Alberta." Ph.D. diss., University of Alberta, 1995.

755. Jackson, Edgar Lionel. *North American Research on Public Attitudes to Energy Resources and Conservation: A Bibliographic Essay.* Working Paper, EPR-10. Toronto, ON: University of Toronto, Institute for Environmental Studies, 1982.

756. Jackson, Edgar Lionel, and Leslie T. Foster. *Energy Attitudes and Policies.* Cornett Occasional Papers, no. 2. Victoria, BC: University of Victoria, Department of Geography, 1980.

757. Jones, Chris F., and Bruce I. McIntyre. *British Columbia Forest Service - Internal Attitude Survey on Pesticide Use.* Pest Management Report. Victoria, BC: Ministry of Forests and Lands, 1987.

758. Keller, Gerald, and Gordon H. G. McDougall. *The Energy Situation: Consumer Attitudes and Reactions (1975 - 1984).* Ottawa, ON: Department of Consumer and Corporate Affairs, Policy Coordination Bureau, 1984.

759. Keller, Gerald, and Gordon H. G. McDougall. *A Survey of the Canadian Public's Attitudes towards the Energy Situation, Vol. II.* Hull, PQ: Consumer and Corporate Affairs Canada, Policy Coordination Bureau, 1984.

760. Kelly, Michael L. *Attitudes toward the Environment: A Comparison of Six Surveys Spanning Six Years.* Edmonton, AB: Environment Council of Alberta, 1982.

761. Kelly, Michael L., and Kim Sanderson. "Sea Changes, Sustainability and Strategies (Changing Attitudes Lead to Different Strategies for Implementing Environmental Policy)." *Alternatives* 16, no. 17 (1990): 30-36.

631. Keenleyside, Terrence A., Lawrence LeDuc, and J. Alex Murray. "Public Opinion and Canada-United States Economic Relations." *Behind the Headlines* 35, no. 4 (1976).

632. Kehoe, Mary. "Job-Entry Discrimination: Survey of Toronto Employers." *Canadian Labour* 30 (1985): 12-15.

633. Kelly, Maria V. *The Relationship between Employment Status and Attitudes regarding Work.* Toronto, ON: Ontario Ministry of Correctional Services, 1981.

634. Kingston, Anne. "Attitudes to Debt Need as Much Overhaul as the Bankruptcy Act." *Financial Times of Canada* 79, no. 52 (1991): 15.

635. Knoop, Robert, and Alexander Sanders. *Furniture Industry: Attitudes towards Exporting.* Technological Innovation Studies Program, Research Report, 44. Ottawa, ON: Industry, Trade and Commerce, Technology Branch, 1978.

636. Krahn, Harvey et al. "Explanations of Unemployment in Canada." *International Journal of Comparative Sociology* 28, no. 3-4 (1987): 228-36.

637. Krahn, Harvey, and Trevor Harrison. "'Self-referenced' Relative Deprivation and Economic Beliefs: The Effects of the Recession in Alberta." *Canadian Review of Sociology and Anthropology* 29, no. 2 (1992): 191-209.

638. Krahn, Harvey, and Graham S. Lowe. "Public Attitudes towards Unions: Some Canadian Evidence." *Journal of Labor Research* 5, no. 2 (1984): 149-64.

639. La Palombara, Joseph, and Stephen Blank. *Multinational Corporations and National Elites: A Study in Tensions.* Conference Board Report, no. 702. New York, NY: Conference Board, 1976.

640. Langford, Tom. "Involvement with Unions, Union Belief Perspectives, and Desires for Union Membership." *Journal of Labor Research* 15, no. 3 (1994): 257-70.

641. Langford, Tom. "Workers' Subordinate Values: A Canadian Case Study." *Canadian Journal of Sociology* 11, no. 3 (1986): 269-91.

642. Lanphier, M. et al. *Analysis of Attitudes toward Unemployment Insurance.* Research Report, ANA. North York, ON: York University, Institute for Behavioural Research, 1970.

643. Larter, Sylvia et al. *Students' Attitudes to Work and Unemployment: Part 2 - The Attitude Questionnaire.* Toronto, ON: Board of Education for the City of Toronto, Research Department, 1978.

644. Larter, Sylvia, and John Fitzgerald. *Students' Attitudes to Work and Unemployment: Pt. 3 - The Open-Ended and True-False Questions.* Toronto, ON: Board of Education for the City of Toronto, Research Department, 1978.

645. LeBrasseur, Roland. "Retirement and Skill Issues in Northern Ontario Industries." *Industrial Relations* 45, no. 2 (1990): 268-80.

646. Leman, Marc. *Canadian-American Relations: Significant Developments.* Current Issue Review, 79-34E. Ottawa, ON: Library of Parliament, Research Branch, 1987.

647. Leroux, P. "Study of Employee Participation and Attitudes of the Recreation Program at the Mutual Life Assurance Company of Canada, Head Office, Waterloo." Master's thesis, University of Waterloo, Department of Recreation, 1978.

648. Lightman, Ernie S. "Economics of Supply of Canada's Military Manpower." *Industrial Relations* 14, no. 2 (1975): 209-19.

649. Lipsey, Richard G., and Murray G. Smith. *Global Imbalances and U.S. Policy Responses: A Canadian Perspective.* Toronto, ON: C. D. Howe Institute; Washington, DC: National Planning Association, 1987.

650. Livingstone, D. W., and Meg Luxton. "Gender Consciousness at Work: Modification of the Male Breadwinner Norm among Steelworkers and Their Spouses." *Canadian Review of Sociology and Anthropology* 26, no. 2 (1989): 240-75.

651. London, Ontario. Committee for International Development. *Report of a Survey of Attitudes of the Citizens of London, Ontario towards International Development.* London, ON: The Committee, 1970.

652. Long, Richard J. "Worker Ownership and Job Attitudes: A Field Study." *Industrial Relations* 21, no. 2 (1982): 196-215.

653. Lowe, Graham S., and Harvey Krahn. "Recent Trends in Public Support for Unions in Canada." *Journal of Labor Research* 10, no. 4 (1989): 391-410.

654. Lowe, Graham S., and Harvey Krahn. "Where Wives Work: The Relative Effects of Situational and Attitudinal Factors." *Canadian Journal of Sociology* 10, no. 1 (1985): 1-22.

655. Luce, Sally R., and Gene R. Swimmer. *Worker Attitudes about Health and Safety in Three Asbestos Break Manufacturing Plants*. Study Series, no. 6. Toronto, ON: Royal Commission on Matters of Health and Safety Arising from the Use of Asbestos in Ontario, 1982.

656. MacCrimmon, Kenneth R., and Donald A. Wehnung. "A Portfolio of Risk Measures." *Theory and Decision* 19, no. 1 (1985): 1-29.

657. Macmillan, Katie. *Women and Free Trade*. Trade Monitor, no. 5. Toronto, ON: C. D. Howe Institute, 1988.

658. Mallen, Bruce E., and Jean Francois Pernotte. *Decision Making and Attitudes of Canadian Freight and Cargo Transportation Buyers*. Montreal, PQ: Sir George Williams University, 1972.

659. Marshall Fenn Ltd. *Study of Attitudes and Levels of Information Relating to the Apprenticeship System*. Toronto, ON: Ontario Ministry of Education, 1976.

660. Marton, Katherin. "Attitudes toward Foreign Investments: A Case Study of the Canadian Blue Collar Worker Employed at Ford Canada." Ph.D. diss., New York University, Graduate School of Business Administration, 1973.

661. Marzolini, Michael, and Peter Carter. "Reflections from the Glass Towers: Executive Survey." *Metropolitan Toronto Business Journal* 80, no. 6 (1990): 27-32.

662. McInnes, David. "And Now - - Consumerism!: Consumer Attitudes Are Having a Bigger Impact on How Banks Do Business." *CGA Magazine* 23, no. 12 (1989): 36-40.

663. McKie, Craig. "American Managers in Canada: A Comparative Profile." *International Journal of Comparative Sociology* 18, no. 1-2 (1977): 44-62.

664. McLaren, K. Louise. "Accommodations: Access to Opportunities." *The Canadian Banker* 97, no. 6 (1990): 58-63.

665. McNeil, Jeannine, and Micheline Garand. *The Effects of Word Processing and Automated Data Entry Technology on the Quantity and Quality of Users' Jobs: Summary*. Laval, PQ: Canadian Workplace Automation Research Centre, Organizational Research Directorate, 1989.

666. McShane, Steven L. "General Union Attitude: A Construct Validation." *Journal of Labor Research* 7, no. 4 (1986): 403-17.

667. Metropolitan Toronto, (Ont.). Transportation Division. *Scarborough Town Centre Light Rail Transit: Survey of Community Attitudes, Report 3*. Toronto, ON: Metropolitan Toronto Planning Department, 1975.

668. Meyer, Katherine. "The Influence of Gender on Work Activities and Attitudes of Senior Civil Servants in the United States, Canada, and Great Britain." *Research in Politics and Society* 2 (1986): 283-99.

669. Murphy, Jean. "Management Survey: What Canada's Chief Executives Are Thinking." *The Financial Post* 83, no. 46 (1989): 63-65.

670. Murray, J. Alex, and Lawrence Leduc. *Cross-Sectional Analysis of Canadian Public Attitudes toward U.S. Equity Investment in Canada*. Working Paper Series, 2/75. Toronto, ON: Ontario Economic Council, 1975.

671. Murray, Michael A., and Tom Atkinson. "Gender Differences in Correlates of Job Satisfaction." *Canadian Journal of Behavioural Science* 13, no. 1 (1981): 44-52.

672. Muszynski, Leon, and David A. Wolfe. "New Technology and Training: Lessons from Abroad." *Canadian Public Policy* 15, no. 3 (1989): 245-64.

673. Nakatsu, C. T. "Attitude of Government and Industry toward the Consumers' Association of Canada." M.Sc. thesis, University of Guelph, 1972.

674. Nelson, Kelly. "Building in Quality: The Actions of Senior Executives Must Demonstrate Their Commitment." *Canadian Business Review* 18, no. 4 (1991): 22-25.

675. Never, D. et al. "Attitudes towards Foreign Products and International Price Competition." *The Canadian Journal of Economics* 24, no. 1 (1991): 1-11.

676. Nightingale, Donald V., and Jean-Marie Toulouse. "Values, Structure, Process, and Reactions/Adjustments: A Comparison of French and English Canadian Industrial Organizations." *Canadian Journal of Behavioural Science* 9, no. 1 (1977): 37-48.

677. Ontario. Legislative Assembly. Select Committee on Economic and Cultural Nationalism, and Kates, Peat, Marwick & Co. *Overview Report; Part of a Study on Foreign Ownership: Corporate Behaviour and Public Attitudes*. [Toronto], ON: The Committee, 1971.

762. Klemanski, John S., and Brent S. Steel. "Citizen Attitudes, Knowledge and Participation in Environmental Policy-Making: Michigan, Ontario, and the Case of Acid Rain." *Michigan Academician* 21, no. 2 (1989): 175-89.

763. Kline, S. *Rationalizing Attitude Discrepant Behaviour: A Case Study in Energy Attitudes.* Faculty Research Paper Series, A. North York, ON: York University, Faculty of Environmental Studies, 1988.

764. Kreutzwiser, R. D., and S. H. Wright. *Municipal Recycling and Household Conservation Behaviour: A Study of Guelph, Ontario: A Report.* Toronto, ON: Ministry of the Environment, 1991.

765. Kuhn, Richard G. "Factors Affecting Energy Preferences: Environmental Attitudes and Reasons for Choice." *The Canadian Geographer* 32, no. 2 (1988): 165-67.

766. Larsen, N. P. J. *The Journey to Twillingate.* Canadian Translation of Fisheries and Aquatic Sciences/Canada. Department of Fisheries and Oceans, no. 5169. Ottawa, ON: National Research Council, Canada Institute for Scientific and Technical Information, 1985.

767. McDougall, Gordon H. G., and Gerald Keller. *Energy: Canadians' Attitudes and Reactions (1975-1980).* Ottawa, ON: Consumer and Corporate Affairs Canada, Consumer Research and Evaluation Branch, 1981.

768. McGovern, Celeste. "Little Green Sprouts: Green Orthodoxy Roots Itself in the School System." *Alberta (Western) Report* 18, no. 21 (1991): 43.

769. McMeiken, J. Elizabeth. *Public Health Professionals and the Environment: A Study of Perceptions and Attitudes.* Social Science Series, 5. Ottawa, ON: Inland Waters Directorate, Water Planning and Management Branch, 1972.

770. Mitchell, Jared. "No Deals: That's the Attitude toward Business of Too Many of Canada's Environmental Guerrillas." *Report on Business Magazine (Globe and Mail)* 6, no. 4 (1989): 72-73, 75+.

771. Nevitte, Neil, and Mebs Kanji. "Explaining Environmental Concern and Action in Canada." *Applied Behavioral Science Review* 3, no. 1 (1995): 85-102.

772. New Brunswick. Department of Municipal Affairs and Environment. *Solid Waste Management in New Brunswick.* Fredericton, NB: The Department, 1989.

773. Ontario. Ministry of Energy, and Canadian Energy Research Institute. *Ontario's Energy Choices Conference: Proceedings*. Toronto, ON: Ontario's Energy Choices Conference, 1989.

774. Ontario Royal Commission on Electric Power Planning. *Ontario Royal Commission on Electric Power Planning - Preliminary Statement on the Current Public Awareness, Attitudes and Expectations*. Toronto, ON: The Commission, 1975.

775. OPTIMA Consultants, and Canada. Environment Canada. Environmental Protection Service. *Attitudes towards Air Pollution and Stricter Vehicle Emission Standards: Results of a National Public Opinion Survey*. Ottawa, ON: Environmental Protection Service, 1985.

776. Patterson, Jeffery. *Green City Views: Public Opinion and Urban Environments in Ten Canadian Cities*. Research and Working Papers, 39. Winnipeg, MB: University of Winnipeg, Institute of Urban Studies, 1995.

777. Rempel, G., and Metropolitan Corporation of Greater Winnipeg, Manitoba Waterworks and Waste Disposal Division. *Consumer Attitude Survey on Water Quality and River Pollution Control*. Winnipeg, MB: Metropolitan Corporation of Greater Winnipeg, Manitoba Waterworks and Waste Disposal Division, 1971.

778. Saskatchewan. Fisheries and Wildlife Branch. *Survey of Farmer Attitudes toward Wildlife, Habitat Retention and Hunting in Saskatchewan*. Regina, SK: Department of Tourism and Renewable Resources, Fisheries and Wildlife Branch, 1978.

779. Self, Burl E. *Public Attitudes regarding Selected Wildlife Issues in British Columbia*. Fish and Wildlife Bulletin, no. B-14. Victoria, BC: Province of British Columbia, Ministry of Environment, 1982.

780. Semper Paratus Limited. *Study of Awareness, Attitudes and Future Expectations of Ontario Residents regarding the Supply and Use of Electric Energy - Vol. 1*. Toronto, ON: Royal Commission on Electric Power Planning, 1976- .

781. Sewell, W. R. Derrick, and Ian Burton. *Perceptions and Attitudes in Resources Management*. Resource Paper, 2. Ottawa, ON: Department of Energy, Mines and Resources, Policy Research and Coordination Branch, 1971.

782. Sharratt, Ken, and Ontario. Ministry of Transportation and Communications. *Motor Oil Recycling: Patterns of Motor Oil Use and Attitudes towards a Re-Refined Product.* Downsview, ON: Ministry of Transportation and Communications, Research and Development Division, 1976.

783. Shulman, Norman. *Public Attitudes and Behaviour Related to Energy Conservation: Report 2 - Survey of Urban Priorities.* Ottawa, ON: Central Mortgage and Housing Corporation, 1979.

784. Smiley, A., and N. P. Moray. *Review of 12-Hour Shifts at Nuclear Generating Stations: Final Report.* Research Report, INFO-0318. Ottawa, ON: Canada Atomic Energy Control Board, 1989.

785. Smith, Geoffrey C., and David Alderdice. "Public Responses to National Park Environmental Policy." *Environment and Behavior* 11, no. 3 (1979): 329-50.

786. Steel, Brent S., and Dennis L. Soden. "Acid Rain Policy in Canada and the United States: Attitudes of Citizens, Environmental Activists, and Legislators." *The Social Science Journal* 26, no. 1 (1989): 27-44.

787. Steger, Mary Ann E. et al. "Political Culture, Postmaterial Values, and the New Environmental Paradigm: A Comparative Analysis of Canada and the United States." *Political Behaviour* 11, no. 3 (1989): 233-54.

788. Steger, Mary Ann E., and Stephanie L. Witt. "Gender Differences in Environmental Orientations: A Comparison of Publics and Activists in Canada and the U.S." *The Western Political Quarterly* 42 (1989): 627-49.

789. Thompson Lightstone & Company Limited. *Public Awareness and Attitudes on Environmental Issues, Focus Groups and In-depth Interviews: Research Report.* Ottawa, ON: Environment Canada, 1990.

790. Wall, Geoffrey, and Leslie Marxheimer. "Attitudes of Backcountry Users to Proposed Management Strategies in Kluane National Park Reserve." *Environments* 20, no. 1 (1989): 82-86.

791. Wall, Glenda. "General versus Specific Environmental Concern: A Western Canadian Case." *Environment and Behavior* 27, no. 3 (1995): 294-316.

792. Watt, Erik. "New Attitude in Mining? (In the North)." *Up Here: Life in Canada's North* 4, no. 5 (1988): 50-52.

793. Winham, Gilbert. "Attitudes on Pollution and Growth in Hamilton, or 'There's an Awful Lot of Talk These Days about Ecology'." *Canadian Journal of Political Science* 5, no. 3 (1972): 389-401.

Section 5

Mass Media

794. Avrim Lazar and Associates. *Attitudes of Canadians toward Advertising on Television*. Ottawa, ON: Canadian Radio-Television and Telecommunications Commission, Research Branch, 1978.

795. Canada. Canadian Radio-Television and Telecommunications Commission. Research Branch. *Attitudes of Canadians toward Advertising on Television*. Hull, PQ: Supply and Services Canada, 1978.

796. Canada. Communications Research Centre, and Ontario. Ministry of Transportation and Communication. Communication Division. *FM Radio Listener and Broadcaster Attitudes*. Toronto, ON: Ontario Ministry of Transportation and Communications, Communications Division; Communications Research Centre, 1985.

797. Canada Market Research, and Ontario. Ministry of Transportation and Communication. *Attitudes of the Public and Small Business to a Cable Classified Advertising Channel, November 1984*. Downsview, ON: Ministry of Transportation and Communications, 1984.

798. Canadian Radio-Television and Telecommunications Commission. Research Branch. *Public Attitudes towards Advertising*. Toronto, ON: Market Facts of Canada, 1975.

799. Check, James V. P. et al. *Survey of Canadians' Attitudes regarding Sexual Content in the Media*. LaMarsh Research Programme Reports on Violence and Conflict Resolution. Downsview, ON: York University, Department of Psychology, 1985.

800. Contemporary Research Centre. *A Comparative Attitudes Study: Magazines - Television*. Toronto, ON: Contemporary Research Centre, 1971.

801. Freeman, Barbara M. "The Media and the Royal Commission on the Status of Women in Canada, 1966-1972: Research in Progress." *Resources for Feminist Research* 23, no. 3 (1994): 3-9.

802. Gorn, Gerald J. et al. "The Role of Educational Television in Changing the Intergroup Attitudes of Children." *Child Development* 47, no. 1 (1976): 277-80.

803. Indra, Doreen Marie. "Ethnicity, Social Stratification, and Opinion Formation: An Analysis of Ethnic Portrayal in the Vancouver Newspaper Press, 1905-1976." Ph.D. diss., Simon Fraser University, 1979.

804. Khaki, Aziz. *Depiction and Perception: Native Indians and Visible Minorities in the Media.* Vancouver, BC: Ad Hoc Committee for Better Race Relations, 1988.

805. Moore, Timothy E., and Leslie Cadeau. "Representation of Women, the Elderly and Minorities in Canadian Television Commercials." *Canadian Journal of Behavioural Science* 17, no. 3 (1985): 215-25.

806. Rich, Tom et al. "What Canadians Disliked about TV Commercials." *Journal of Advertising Research* 18, no. 6 (1978): 37-44.

807. Samarajiwa, Rohan et al. "The Politics of Culture and Information: Kent and Applebert in Review." *Studies in Political Economy* 12 (Fall 1983): 121-52.

808. Surlin, Stuart H., and Eugene D. Tate. "'All in the Family': Is Archie Funny?" *Journal of Communication* 26, no. 4 (1976): 61-68.

809. Weatherbe, Steve. "Media's Message: A New Study Finds An Anti-Free Trade Slant in Both the Globe and the CBC." *Alberta (Western) Report* 15, no. 46 (1988): 26-28.

Section 6

Public Policy

810. Ahmed, Sadrudin A. *Psychographics for Social Policy Decisions: A Case of Attitudes Relating to Welfare Assistance*. London, ON: University of Western Ontario, Department of Psychology, 1977.

811. Alberta Association of Municipal Districts and Counties, and Alberta Urban Municipalities Association. *Municipal Attitudes towards Regional Planning in Alberta: Attitudes of Selected Urban and Rural Municipalities on Regional Planning Agencies in Alberta*. Toronto, ON: Micromedia, 1980.

812. Alberta Community Development. *Government Releases Research Findings*. Edmonton, AB: Alberta Community Development, 1995.

813. Alberta Education, Policy and Planning Branch. *Alberta Children and Youth: Trends and Issues, 1995*. Edmonton, AB: The Branch, 1996.

814. Atkinson, Michael M., and William Donald Coleman. "Bureaucrats and Politicians in Canada: An Examination of the Political Administration Model." *Comparative Political Studies* 18 (1985): 58-80.

815. Bozinoff, Lorne, and Peter MacIntosh. *Dramatic Reversal in Attitudes Concerning Defence Spending*. Toronto, ON: Gallup Canada, 1989.

816. Bryant, Alan W. "Public Attitudes toward the Exclusion of Evidence: Section 24(2) of the Canadian Charter of Rights and Freedoms." *Canadian Bar Review* 69, no. 1 (1990): 1-45.

817. Bull, Shelley B. et al. "Restrictions on Smoking: Growth in Population Support between 1983 and 1991 in Ontario, Canada." *Journal of Public Health Policy* 15 (Autumn 1994): 310-28.

818. Canada. Task Force on Broadcasting Policy. *Report of the Task Force on Broadcasting Policy*. Toronto, ON: Minister of Supply and Services Canada, 1986.

819. Canadian Institute of International Affairs et al. *Public Consultation on Population Questions: A Report to the Government of Canada*. Toronto, ON: Canadian Institute of International Affairs, 1974.

820. Carson, Bruce. *The Charter of Rights: Fundamental Freedoms and Mobility Rights*. Current Issue Review, 84-16E. Ottawa, ON: Library of Parliament, Research Branch, 1987.

821. Coughlin, Richard M. "Social Policy and Ideology: Public Opinion in Eight Rich Nations." *Comparative Social Research* 2 (1979): 3-40.

822. Driedger, Michael, Don Munton, and Canadian Institute for International Peace and Security. *The 1988 CIIPS Public Opinion Survey: Security, Arms Control and Defence: Public Attitudes in Canada*. Ottawa, ON: Canadian Institute for International Peace and Security, 1988.

823. Fletcher, Frederick J. *Canadian Attitude Trends, 1960-1978*. Montreal, PQ: Institute for Research on Public Policy, 1979.

824. Forbes, J. D. "Comments on 'Causes and Intervention in Canadian Agriculture'; 'Policy Processes in the Canadian Agricultural-Agribusiness Sector': Review Article." *Canadian Journal of Agricultural Economics* 38, no. 4 (1990): 801-2.

825. Gibson, Gordon. *Plan B: The Future of the Rest of Canada*. Vancouver, BC: Fraser Institute, 1994.

826. Howard, Rhoda. "The Canadian Government Response to Africa's Refugee Problem." *Canadian Journal of African Studies* 15, no. 1 (1981): 95-116.

827. Jabes, Jak. "Qualitative Results: 1988 Survey of Management Attitudes in the Federal Government." *Optimum* 20, no. 2 (1989): 25-37.

828. Johnston, Richard. *Public Opinion and Public Policy in Canada: Questions of Confidence*. Collected Research Studies, 35. Toronto, ON: University of Toronto Press, 1986.

829. Knuttila, K. Murray, and James N. McCorie. "National Policy and Prairie Agrarian Development: A Reassessment." *Canadian Review of Sociology and Anthropology* 17, no. 3 (1980): 263-72.

830. Labonte, Richard. "Healthy Public Policy in Canada: A Survey of Ontario Health Professionals." *International Quarterly of Community Health Education* 9, no. 4 (1988-89): 321-42.

831. Laframboise, Josette. *A Question of Needs*. Ottawa, ON: Canadian Council on Social Development, 1975.

832. Leman, Marc. *Canadian Multiculturalism*. Current Issue Review. Ottawa, ON: Library of Parliament, Research Branch, 1994.

833. Mackay, Harry. *National Opinion Polls on Social Development, June 1987 and March 1988*. Ottawa, ON: Canadian Council on Social Development, 1988.

834. Mauser, Gary A. "A Comparison of Canadian and American Attitudes towards Firearms." *Canadian Journal of Criminology* 32, no. 4 (1990): 573-89.

835. McQueen, David. "MP's Pay: The Rip-off that Wasn't [Questions Widely Held Canadian Beliefs Concerning the 1981 Increase in Pay of Members of Parliament]." *Canadian Public Policy* 8 (Autumn 1982): 554-60.

836. Munton, Don. *The 1990 CIIPS Public Opinion Survey: Changing Conceptions of Security: Public Attitudes in Canada*. Ottawa, ON: Canadian Institute for International Peace and Security, 1990.

837. Murray, J. Alex, and Lawrence LeDuc. "Public Opinion and Foreign Policy Options in Canada." *Public Opinion Quarterly* 40, no. 4 (1976): 488-96.

838. National Technology Policy Roundtable. Manitoba Workshop (1989: Winnipeg, Man.). *The Technology Engine in Community Economic Development: Proceedings*. Winnipeg, MB: Winnipeg Business Development Corporation; Manitoba Industry, Trade and Tourism, 1989.

839. Northwest Territories. Affirmative Action Policy Review Task Group. *Report on the Consultation Findings of the Affirmative Action Policy Review Task Group*. Yellowknife, NT: The Task Group, 1995.

840. Ontario Advisory Committee on Liquor Regulation. *Report of the Advisory Committee on Liquor Regulation*. Toronto, ON: The Committee, 1987.

841. Ottawa. Department of External Affairs. *Canadians' Foreign Policy Attitudes*. Communique, 87/162. Ottawa, ON: The Department, 1987.

842. Pereira, Cecil. "Canadian Beliefs and Policy regarding the Admission of Ugandan Asians to Canada." *Ethnic and Racial Studies* 1, no. 3 (1978): 352-64.

843. Reudig, Wolfgang. "Outcomes of Nuclear Technology Policy: Do Varying Political Styles Make a Difference?" *Journal of Public Policy* 7 (1987): 389-430.

844. Rubin, Don. "Viewpoint." *Performing Arts in Canada* 26, no. 1 (1990): 46.

845. Sniderman, Paul M. et al. "Political Culture and the Problem of Double Standards: Mass and Elite Attitudes toward Language Rights in the Canadian Charter of Rights and Freedom." *Canadian Journal of Political Science* 22, 23 (1990): 259-84, 531-44.

846. Tisdall, Paul. *Innovation and Intellectual Property Rights in Canada*. Discussion Paper. Ottawa, ON: Science Council of Canada, 1990.

847. Vercammen, James, and Murray Fulton. "The Economic Implications of Farm Interest Groups' Beliefs." *American Journal of Agricultural Economics* 72, no. 4 (1990): 851-63.

848. Williams, A. Paul. *Elite Attitudes toward Canadian Social Welfare Policy*. Downsview, ON: York University, Institute for Behavioural Research, 1982.

Section 7

Lifestyle Issues

849. Alberta. Alberta Community Development, Alberta. Alberta Education, and Alberta. Human Rights Commission. *A Survey of Attitudes toward Human Rights and toward Self in Alberta Schools: Technical Report*. Edmonton, AB: Community Development; Alberta Education; Human Rights Commission, 1992.

850. Alberta. Alberta Transportation. *Alberta Drivers' Attitudes Survey, September 1981*. Edmonton, AB: MIR Information Research, 1981.

851. Alberta. Department of Tourism and Small Business. *Profile of the Alberta Visitor: A Study of Their Attitudes and Motivations - Results of Stage 1*. Edmonton, AB: Travel Alberta, 1983.

852. Albinson, J. G. "Professionalized Attitudes of Volunteer Coaches toward Playing a Game." *International Review of Sport Sociology* 8, no. 2 (1973): 77-87.

853. Anderson, Grace M., and J. M. Alleyne. "Ethnicity, Food Preferences and Habits of Consumption as Factors in Social Interaction." *Canadian Ethnic Studies* 11, no. 1 (1979): 83-87.

854. Arlett, Alan et al. *Canada Gives: Trends and Attitudes towards Charitable Giving and Voluntarism 1988*. Toronto, ON: Canadian Center for Philanthropy, 1988.

855. Atkinson, Tom. "Changing Attitudes toward Work in Canada: Advancement Opportunities and Influence on Decision-Making, Rather than Pay Scales, Have Caused Declining Job Satisfaction among Most Groups of Employees." *Canadian Business Review* 10 (Spring 1983): 39-44.

856. Axworthy, Tom. *Our American Cousins: The United States through Canadian Eyes*. Toronto, ON: J. Lorimer, 1987.

857. Baer, Douglas E. et al. "Respect for Authority in Canada." *Sociological Focus* 28, no. 2 (1995): 177-95.

858. Baer, Douglas E. et al. *The Three Nations of North America? National Character, Regional Culture, and the Values of Canadians and Americans*. Research Discussion Paper, no. 87. Edmonton, AB: University of Alberta, Department of Sociology, 1992.

859. Baseline Market Research. *Sunday Shopping Survey: Final Report*. Fredericton, NB: Department of Municipalities, Culture and Housing, 1992.

860. Battles, Robert Anthony Marvin. "Townhouses in Single Family Areas: An Analysis of Public Attitudes towards Increasing Density." Master's thesis, University of British Columbia, 1976.

861. BC Stats. *British Columbia Highlights of the Youth Smoking Survey*. Victoria, BC: BC Stats, 1996.

862. Belanger, J. D. *Unemployment Insurance: Decisions Involving the Act and the Charter*. Rev ed. Canada Library of Parliament, Background Paper, BP-191E. Ottawa, ON: Library of Parliament, Research Branch, 1992.

863. Bemmels, Brian, and Yonatan Reshef. "Manufacturing Employees and Technological Change." *Journal of Labor Research* 12 (Summer 1991): 231-46.

864. Bennett, Lorna R., and Doreen Westera. "The Primacy of Relationships for Teens: Issues and Responses." *Family and Community Health* 17, no. 3 (1994): 60-69.

865. Bergob, Michael J. "Nomothetic Militancy toward Alcohol Use among Abstainers." *Social Science Journal* 31, no. 4 (1994): 335-54.

866. Brinkerhoff, Merlin B., and Jeffrey C. Jacob. "Alternative Technology and Quality of Life: An Exploratory Survey of British Columbia Smallholders." *Social Indicators Research* 14, no. 2 (1984): 177-94.

867. British Columbia. Ministry of Economic Development. *The British Columbia Alpine Skier Survey, 1985-86*. Victoria, BC: The Ministry, 1987.

868. Burke, Ronald J. "Stress, Satisfaction and Militancy among Canadian Physicians." *Industrial Relations* 50, no. 3 (1995): 617-35.

869. Bylok, J. et al. *Seat Belt Usage and Driver Attitude Survey, May 1981: A Summary Report*. Downsview, ON: Ontario Ministry of Transportation and Communications, Policy Planning and Research Division, 1981.

870. C. Thomas Hathaway Associates, and British Columbia. Ministry of Labour and Consumer Services. *A Survey of B.C. Population Attitudes, Knowledge and Behaviour regarding Drinking and Driving*. Victoria, BC: Ministry of Labour and Consumer Services, 1989.

871. Callister, Lynn Clark et al. "Cultural Perceptions of Childbirth: A Cross-Cultural Comparison of Childbearing Women." *Journal of Holistic Nursing* 14, no. 1 (1996): 66-78.

872. Campbell Goodell Consultants Limited, British Columbia. Ministry of Municipal Affairs. Recreation and Culture, and British Columbia. Ministry of Tourism and Provincial Secretary. *British Columbia Heritage Site Visitor Survey*. Victoria, BC: Ministry of Municipal Affairs, Recreation and Culture, 1989.

873. Canada. Canadian Government Office of Tourism. *Tracking Study of Attitudes towards Vacation Travel among Residents of Seven Cities in Canada 1978-1979 (Documentation 1 Codebook, 2 Questionnaires, 1 Study Description)*. Ottawa, ON: Canadian Government Office of Tourism, 1979.

874. Canada. Health and Welfare Canada, and Canada. Transport Canada. *National Survey on Drinking and Driving, 1988: Technical Report*. Ottawa, ON: Health and Welfare Canada; Transport Canada, 1992.

875. Canada Mortgage and Housing Corporation. *Downtown Eastside Housing and Residents Surveys, 1987-88*. Vancouver, BC: The Corporation, 1989.

876. Canada. National Advisory Council on Aging. *The NACA Position on the Image of Aging*. Aging and NACA, 14. Ottawa, ON: The Council, 1993.

877. Canada. Office of Tourism. Marketing Research Office. *Report on Vacation Attitudes and Vacation Patterns of Canadians, 1973 and the Canadian Travel Agent, 1974*. Ottawa, ON: Office of Tourism, Marketing Research Office, 1975.

878. Canada Roads and Motor Vehicle Traffic Safety Branch, and Ruth M. Heron. *Review of Three Studies Attempting to Relate Reported Seat Belt Usage to Seat Belt Attitudes and Other Variables*. Ottawa, ON: Transport Canada, Road and Motor Vehicle Traffic Safety Branch, 1975.

879. Canada. Royal Commission on New Reproductive Technologies. *Proceed with Care: Final Report*. Ottawa, ON: The Commission, 1993.

880. Canada. Royal Commission on New Reproductive Technologies. *Social Values and Attitudes Surrounding New Reproductive Technologies*. Research Studies, 2. Ottawa, ON: The Commission, 1993.

881. Canada. Tourism Canada. *Canadian Tourism Attitude and Motivation Study*. Ottawa, ON: Tourism Canada, 1984.

882. Chochinov, Harvey Max, and Keith G. Wilson. "The Euthanasia Debate: Attitudes, Practices and Psychiatric Considerations." *Canadian Journal of Psychiatry* 40, no. 10 (1995): 593-602.

883. Cohen, Aaron. "An Examination of the Relationships between Work Commitment and Nonwork Domains." *Human Relations* 48, no. 3 (1995): 239-63.

884. Cote, James E. "Traditionalism and Feminism: A Typology of Strategies Used by University Women to Manage Career-Family Conflicts." *Social Behavior and Personality* 14, no. 2 (1986): 133-43.

885. Crawford, Craig, and James E. Curtis. "English Canadian-American Differences in Value Orientations: Survey Comparisons Bearing on Lipset's Thesis." *Studies in Comparative International Development* 14, no. 3-4 (1979): 23-44.

886. Curtis, James E., and Richard Ennis. "Negative Consequences of Leaving Competitive Sport?: Comparative Findings for Former Elite-Level Hockey Players." *Sociology of Sport Journal* 5, no. 2 (1988): 87-106.

887. Decima Research Ltd. "Study Shows Technophobia Declining among Canadians." *Computing Canada* 19, no. 25 (1993): 2.

888. Dickinson, Harley et al. "Women's Health, Labor Force Participation, and Lifestyles: Selected Findings from the 1985 General Social Survey, Canada." *International Journal of Contemporary Sociology* 29, no. 2 (1992): 163-86.

889. Ekos Research Associates Inc. "Privacy Study Reveals a Fear of Computers." *Computing Canada* 19, no. 8 (1993): 1,6.

890. Energy Pathways Inc. *Consumer Housing Choices and the Environment*. Ottawa, ON: Canada Mortgage and Housing Corporation, Research Division, 1991.

891. England, Claire St. Clere. "The Climate of Censorship in Ontario: An Investigation into Attitudes toward Intellectual Freedom and the Perceptual Factors Affecting the Practice of Censorship in Public Libraries Serving Medium-Sized Populations." Ph.D. diss., University of Toronto, 1974.

892. Environics Research Group. *Report on the Quality of Life in the GTA, Phase 2: Attitudinal Study*. Toronto, ON: Greater Toronto Coordinating Committee, 1995.

893. Fast, Janet E., and Brenda Munro. "Value of Household and Farm Work: Evidence from Alberta Farm Family Data." *Canadian Journal of Agricultural Economics* 39 (March 1991): 137-50.

894. Flaherty, M. S. "Rural Nonfarm Residential Development: An Examination of Resident Attitudes and Severance Policy Preferences." Master's thesis, University of Guelph, 1978.

895. Fletcher, Frederick J., and R. J. Drummond. *Canadian Attitude Trends, 1960-1978*. Institute for Research on Public Policy Working Paper, 1980-3898. Montreal, PQ: Micromedia; Institute for Research on Public Policy, 1979.

896. Fletcher, Joseph F. "Mass and Elite Attitudes about Wiretapping in Canada: Implications for Democratic Theory and Politics." *Public Opinion Quarterly* 53, no. 2 (1989): 225-45.

897. Friedmann, Karl Anton. *Complaining: Comparative Aspects of Complaint Behavior and Attitudes toward Complaining in Canada and Britain*. Sage Professional Papers in Administration and Policy Studies, ser. no. 03-019. Beverly Hills, CA: Sage Publications, 1974.

898. Geros, Dean R. "Old Principles, New Problems: A Survey of Resident Attitudes in Four Burnaby Neighbourhoods." Ph.D. diss., Queen's University, 1996.

899. Glenday, Daniel. "What Has Work Done to the Working Class? A Comparison of Workers and Production Technologies." *British Journal of Sociology* 46, no. 3 (1995): 475-98.

900. Grabb, Edward G., and S. L. Waugh. "Family Background, Socioeconomic Attainment, and the Ranking of Self-Actualization Values." *Sociological Focus* 20, no. 3 (1987): 215-26.

901. Graves, F. L. et al. *Privacy Revealed: The Canadian Privacy Survey*. Ottawa, ON: Ekos Research Associates, 1993.

902. Graves, F. L., and B. L. Kinsley. *Culture in Canada Today: Issues and Attitudes*. Ottawa, ON: Government of Canada, Department of Communications, Arts and Culture, Research and Statistics, 1982.

903. Greater Vancouver Regional District, B.C. Planning Department. *Brookside Townhouse Development: Survey of Resident Attitudes*. Vancouver, BC: Cornerstone Planning Group, 1977.

904. Greater Vancouver Regional District, B.C. Planning Department. *Survey of Resident Attitudes - Willow Place Urban Townhouses*. Vancouver, BC: The Department, 1978.

905. Gregory, C. Jane, and Brian M. Petrie. "Superstitions of Canadian Intercollegiate Athletes: An Inter-Sport Comparison." *International Review of Sport Sociology* 10, no. 2 (1975): 59-68.

906. Hemsley, G., and D. Duncan. *Seat Belt Usage and Driver Attitude Survey, May / June 1984*. Downsview, ON: Ministry of Transportation and Communications, Policy Planning and Research Division, 1985.

907. Junean, Pierre. *Canadian and U.S. Attitudes to Culture: Some Comparative Observations - An Address by Pierre Juneau to the Canada-U.S. Seminar Series, Center for International Affairs, Harvard University, Cambridge, Mass., Apr. 1, '86*. N.p., 1986.

908. Kaynak, E., and A. Meidan. "Home Buying Behaviour: A Comparison of Canadian vs. British Attitudes." *Management International Review* 20, no. 4 (1980): 53-63.

909. Killorn, J. G. *Prince Edward Island Alcohol and Other Drugs Survey: Highlights Report*. Charlottetown, PE: Addiction Services of P.E.I.; Ottawa, ON: Health Services and Promotion Branch, Health Promotion Directorate, 1991.

910. Klippenstein, D. H., and R. G. Ironside. "Farmers' Attitudes toward Farm-Based Recreational Facilities in Alberta." *Canadian Journal of Agricultural Economics* 21, no. 3 (1973): 23-33.

911. Knoop, Robert. "Relationships among Job Involvement, Job Satisfaction and Organizational Commitment for Nurses." *Journal of Psychology* 129, no. 6 (1995): 643-49.

912. Lalonde, K. G. *Roadside Seat Belt Attitude Survey, May 1977*. Toronto, ON: Ministry of Transportation and Communications, Research and Development Division, 1978.

913. Lero, D. S. *110 Canadian Statistics on Work and Family*. Ottawa, ON: Canadian Advisory Council on the Status of Women, 1994.

914. Longwoods Research Group, and Ontario. Ministry of Housing. *The Longwoods Report on Housing: Public Attitudes and Perceptions of Housing in Ontario*. Toronto, ON: Longwoods Research Group, 1981.

915. Maggs, Jennifer L. et al. "Risky Business: The Paradoxical Meaning of Problem Behavior for Young Adolescents." *Journal of Early Adolescence* 15, no. 3 (1995): 344-62.

916. Marktrend Marketing Research Inc., and British Columbia. Ministry of Tourism. *The Alberta Resident Travel Attitude and Motivation Study*. Victoria, BC: Ministry of Tourism, 1985.

917. Marktrend Marketing Research Inc., and British Columbia. Ministry of Tourism. *Summary of the Alberta Resident Travel Attitude and Motivation Study.; Alberta Resident Travel Study - Summary. TIO*. Victoria, BC: Ministry of Tourism, 1985.

918. Marshall, Diane, and Benjamin Schlesinger. "Communal Family Living: A Canadian Alternative." *Social Science* 53, no. 4 (1978): 217-19.

919. Maxwell, Grant. *Project Feedback: Attitudes at the Canadian Grassroots; Signs and Portents in the Seventies*. Ottawa, ON: Canadian Catholic Conference, 1975-1976.

920. McCarrey, Michael. "Work and Personal Values of Canadian Anglophones and Francophones: Implications for Organizational Behaviour." *Canadian Psychology* 29, no. 1 (1988): 69-83.

921. McNeal, Hildebrand & Associates. *Executive Summary of a Study of Community Attitudes and Social Concerns in the Vancouver Lower Mainland*. Vancouver, BC: Transport Canada, 1979.

922. McPherson, B., and Neil Guppy. "Pre-retirement Life-style and the Degree of Planning for Retirement." *Journal of Gerontology* 32, no. 2 (1979): 254-63.

923. Minch, Candice P. *Manitoba Roadside Survey of Night-Time Driving Behavior: A Report*. Winnipeg, MB: N.p., 1988.

924. Mitchell, S. *Raising the Issues: A Discussion Paper on Aging Women in Ontario*. Toronto, ON: Ontario Advisory Council on Women's Issues, 1991.

925. Munro, Brenda, and Gerald R. Adams. "Love American Style: A Test of Role Structure Theory on Changes in Attitudes toward Love." *Human Relations* 31, no. 3 (1978): 215-28.

926. Neil Griggs and Associates, and Canada Mortgage and Housing Corporation. *Institutional Impediments to the Construction of Detached Small Lot Housing*. Ottawa, ON: Canada Mortgage and Housing Corporation, c1984.

927. Newman, Otto. "The Ideology of Social Problems: Gambling, a Case Study." *Canadian Review of Sociology and Anthropology* 12, no. 4 (1975): 541-50.

928. Noble, Joey. "'Class-ifying' the Poor: Toronto Charities 1850-1880." *Studies in Political Economy* 2 (1979): 109-28.

929. Northcott, Herbert C. "Public Perceptions of the Population Aging 'Crisis'." *Canadian Public Policy* 20, no. 1 (1994): 66-77.

930. Nova Scotia. Department of Development. Mainstreet Program. *Downtown Parking Issues and Insights: 1982 Parking Survey: The Results and Analysis of Results from a Questionnaire Survey Sampling the Attitudes of Downtown Business Groups towards Parking and Related Parking*. Halifax, NS: Department of Development, Mainstreet Program, 1982.

931. Nova Scotia. Halifax Task Force on Pedestrian Safety. *Strategic Planning Report on Pedestrian Safety: Executive Summary*. Halifax, NS: Department of Transportation and Communications, 1989.

932. Ontario Arts Council. *The Arts and the Quality of Life: The Attitudes of Ontarians*. Toronto, ON: Ontario Arts Council, 1995.

933. Ontario. Ministry of Energy. *Monitoring of R-2000 Low Energy Houses, 1986*. Toronto, ON: The Ministry, 1986.

934. Ontario. Premier's Council on Health, Well-Being and Social Justice, and Insight Canada Research. *Aspirations Project: Qualitative Research Report*. Toronto, ON: Insight Canada Research, 1993.

935. Ontario. Premier's Council on Health, Well-Being and Social Justice. *Yours, Mine and Ours: Ontario's Children and Youth, Phase One*. Toronto, ON: The Council, 1994.

936. Ontario Special Committee for the Arts. *Report to the Honourable Susan Fish the Minister of Citizenship and Culture: Vol. 3 Public Survey: Perceptions, Attitudes and Behaviour of Ontario Residents toward the Arts in the Province, 1983*. Ottawa, ON: Ministry of Citizenship and Culture, 1984.

937. Pfeiffer, Martin. "An Examination of Inglehart's Silent Revolution Thesis in Canada." Ph.D. diss., York University, 1992.

938. Pratt, Geraldine. "Housing Tenure and Social Cleavages in Urban Canada." *Annals of the Association of American Geographers* 76 (1986): 366-80.

939. Prentice, Barry E. *Perceptions of Large Trucks by Canadian Drivers*. Research Bulletin, no. 6. Winnipeg, MB: University of Manitoba, Transport Institute, 1989.

940. Prince Edward Island. Department of Tourism and Parks, and Prince Edward Island. Department of Regional Industrial Expansion. *1988 Resident Tourism Attitude Survey*. Charlottetown, PE: Department of Tourism and Parks; Department of Regional Industrial Expansion, 1989.

941. Prince Edward Island. Department of Tourism and Parks, and Prince Edward Island. Department of Regional Industrial Expansion. *Prince Edward Island 1987 Tourist Exit Survey: May 15-October 31*. Charlottetown, PE: Department of Tourism and Parks; Department of Regional Industrial Expansion, 1988.

942. Reker, Gary T., and Edward J. Peacock. "The Life Attitude Profile (LAP): A Multidimensional Instrument for Assessing Attitudes toward Life." *Canadian Journal of Behavioural Science* 13, no. 3 (1981): 264-73.

943. Roberts, Ron. "Back to Nature: Hip Communities." *LSU-Journal of Sociology* 1, no. 1 (1971): 84-103.

944. Royal Commission on the Future of the Toronto Waterfront (Canada). *A Green Strategy for the Greater Toronto Waterfront: Background and Issues: A Discussion Paper*. Report. Toronto, ON: The Commission, 1990.

945. Rusk, B. M., and Canada. Office of Tourism. *Relating Vacation Travel by Canadians to Their Attitude to Canadian and U.S. Vacation Destinations - Paper Delivered to the Working Group in Tourism and Recreation, International Geographers Union, Trent University, Peterborough, Ontario*. Ottawa, ON: Office of Tourism, Marketing Research Office, 1974.

946. Ruston/Tomany and Associates Ltd. *Winnipeg Public Attitude Survey.* Winnipeg, MB: Winnipeg Development Plan Review, 1979.

947. Ruston/Tomany and Associates Ltd., and Travel Alberta. *Rocky Mountain National Parks Utilization Study, Stage I: Visitor Use and Profile Survey Report, v. 1 Executive Summary.* Toronto, ON: Ruston-Tomany and Associates, 1989.

948. Santa-Barbara, J. et al. *Ontario Driver's Knowledge of and Attitudes toward the Demerit Point System.* Downsview, ON: Ontario Ministry of Transportation and Communications, Policy Planning and Research Division, 1981.

949. Saskatchewan. Saskatchewan Health, Saskatchewan Government Insurance, and Saskatchewan. Saskatchewan Justice. *Consultations with Saskatchewan Youth on Health and Safety Issues.* Regina, SK: Province of Saskatchewan, 1994.

950. Sawchuk, Kim. "A Tale of Inscription/Fashion Statements." *Canadian Journal of Political and Social Theory* 11, no. 1-2 (1987): 51-67.

951. Science Council of Canada, and Canada. Ministry of State, Science and Technology. *Public Awareness of Science and Technology in Canada: Report.* Ottawa, ON: Science Council of Canada, 1991.

952. Slack, Trevor, and Lucie Thibault. "Values and Beliefs: Their Role in the Structuring of National Sport Organizations." *Review (ARENA: Institute for Sport and Social Analysis)* 12, no. 2 (1988): 140-55.

953. Smit, B. *Rural Residential Development in Eramosa Township: A Pilot Survey of Trends and Attitudes.* Publication, 99. Guelph, ON: University of Guelph, Centre for Resources Development, 1979.

954. Smith, Michael D. "Hockey Violence: A Test of the Violent Subculture Hypothesis." *Social Problems* 27, no. 2 (1979): 235-47.

955. Smith, Michael D. "Precipitants of Crowd Violence." *Sociological Inquiry* 48, no. 2 (1978): 121-31.

956. Smith, Michael D. "Towards an Explanation of Hockey Violence: A Reference Other Approach." *Canadian Journal of Sociology* 4, no. 2 (1979): 105-24.

957. Smith, Stephen. *Market Research and the Canadian Tourism Attitude and Motivation Study: A Demonstration of the Flexibility of the CTAMS Data Set: Final Report.* Waterloo, ON: Department of Recreation and Leisure Studies, Institute for Tourism Research, 1988.

958. Snider, Earle L. "Explaining Life Satisfaction: It's the Elderly's Attitudes That Count." *Social Science Quarterly* 2, no. 61 (1980): 253-63.

959. Snowball, Laura C., and James R. Robertson. *Tobacco Smoking*. Current Issue Review, 86-22E. Ottawa, ON: Library of Parliament, Research Branch, 1996.

960. Srinivas, Kalburgi M. "Our Changing Work Environment [Occupational Structure and Work Attitudes in Canada]." *The Canadian Banker* 85 (May/June 1978): 40-45.

961. Thomlert, Ian Douglas. "Attitudes, Values and Beliefs of Personnel Serving Persons with Disabilities: A Research to Practice Challenge." Ph.D. diss., University of Victoria, 1995.

962. Thorkelsson Architects Ltd. *Technology Transfer in Housing in Alberta*. Edmonton, AB: Alberta Municipal Affairs, Housing Division, Financial Assistance and Research Branch, 1988.

963. Torrance, Judy. "The Response of Canadian Governments to Violence." *Canadian Journal of Political Science* 10, no. 3 (1977): 473-96.

964. Vaillancourt, Francois, and Micheline Payette. "The Supply of Volunteer Work: The Case of Canada." *Journal of Voluntary Action Research* 15, no. 4 (1986): 45-56.

965. Vaz, Edmund W. *The Professionalization of Young Hockey Players*. Lincoln, NE: University of Nebraska Press, 1982.

966. Vaz, Edmund W. "What Price Victory? An Analysis of Minor Hockey League Players' Attitudes towards Winning." *International Review of Sport Sociology* 9, no. 2 (1974): 33-55.

967. Vinje, I., and K. Huebert. *An Overview of Campus Alcohol Use and Prevention Programs*. Edmonton, AB: Alberta Alcohol and Drug Abuse Commission; Alberta Family Life and Substance Abuse Foundation; Association of Canadian Distillers, 1993.

968. Vuorinen, S. S. "Comparison of Brazilian and Canadian Attitudes towards Helping." Master's thesis, University of Waterloo, 1971.

969. Weston, J. R., and C. Kristen. *Teleconferencing: A Comparison of Attitudes, Uncertainty and Interpersonal Atmospheres in Mediated and Face to Face Group Interaction: Report*. Ottawa, ON: Department of Communications, 1973.

970. Wharton, J. D., and H. R. Harmatz. "An Exploratory Investigation of How Cultural Attitudes Relate to Life Insurance Holdings: A Cross-Cultural Comparison." *Journal of Economic Psychology* 10, no. 2 (1989): 217-27.

971. Wilden, Anthony. *The Imaginary Canadian*. Vancouver, BC: Pulp Press, 1980.

972. Wilson, R. Jean. *National Household Survey on Drinking and Driving: Knowledge Attitudes and Behavior of Canadian Drivers: A Report.* Ottawa, ON: Road Safety and Motor Vehicle Directorate, 1984.

973. York University. Institute for Behavioural Research. *Social Change in Canada: Trends in Attitudes, Values and Perceptions - National Cross-Sectional Survey May-July, 1977.* Downsview, ON: The Institute, 1977.

974. Yukon Territory. Bureau of Statistics. *Yukon Alcohol and Drug Survey, Vol. 1: Technical Report.* Whitehorse, YT: Yukon Government, Executive Council Office, Bureau of Statistics, 1991.

Section 8

Political Attitudes and Behaviour

975. "Attitudes of Canadians toward the Middle East Conflict: Highlights of a National Survey." *Arab Studies Quarterly* 5 (Summer 1983): 292-96.

976. "Canadians Believe Mulroney Means 'Business'." *Canadian Labour* 32, no. 2 (1987): 3.

977. "(P.E.I. Human Rights) Act Called Too Vague: PEI Court Throws Out Political Protections (Provision Prohibiting Discrimination on the Basis of Political Belief)." *Canadian Human Rights Advocate* 4, no. 5 (1988): 5.

978. "When It Comes to Politics, Most Canadians Are Bystanders: Financial Times/Decima Poll." *Financial Times of Canada* 76, no. 40 (1988): 3.

979. Aitken, John. *Conversations: The Diary of a Worried Journalist's Trek across a Divided and Threatened Canada*. Scarborough, ON: Prentice-Hall of Canada, 1978.

980. Amyot, Pierre Raymond. "Factors of Integrative Attitudes in French Canada." Ph.D. diss., Northwestern University, 1970.

981. Archer, Keith. "The Failure of the New Democratic Party: Unions, Unionists, and Politics in Canada." *Canadian Journal of Political Science* 18 (June 1985): 353-66.

982. Archer, Keith. "A Simultaneous Equation Model of Canadian Voting Behaviour." *Canadian Journal of Political Science* 20 (1987): 553-72.

983. Archer, Keith, and Alan Whitehorn. "Opinion Structure among New Democratic Party Activists: A Comparison with Liberals and Conservatives." *Canadian Journal of Political Science* 23, no. 1 (1990): 101-13.

984. Arnason, Robert J. "Attitudes to American Military Bases: The Canadian Case and the Icelandic Model." Master's thesis, Queen's University, 1981.

985. Atkinson, Michael M., and Maureen Mancuso. "Do We Need a Code of
     Conduct for Politicians? The Search for an Elite Political Culture
     of Corruption in Canada." *Canadian Journal of Political Science*
     18, no. 3 (1985): 459-80.

986. Bashevkin, Sylvia B. "Social Change and Political Partisanship: The
     Development of Women's Attitudes in Quebec, 1965-1979."
     Comparative Political Studies 16 (1983): 147-72.

987. Bashevkin, Sylvia B. "Solitudes in Collision? Pan-Canadian and
     Quebec Nationalist Attitudes in the Late 1970s." *Comparative
     Political Studies* 23 (1990): 3-24.

988. Bashevkin, Sylvia B. *Toeing the Lines: Women and Party Politics in
     English Canada*. Toronto, ON: University of Toronto Press, 1985.

989. Black, Hawley. "What Your MP Thinks about Your Problems [Based on
     a Survey of the Attitudes of Canadian Members of Parliament
     toward Business]." *Canadian Business* 53 (1980): 68-73+.

990. Blais, Andre et al. "The Public/Private Sector Cleavage in North
     America: The Political Behavior and Attitudes of Public Sector
     Employees." *Comparative Political Studies* 23 (1990): 381- 403.

991. Blais, Andre, and E. Gidengil. *Making Representative Democracy Work:
     The Views of Canadians*. Canada Royal Commission on Electoral
     Reform and Party Financing, Research Studies, vol. 17. Toronto,
     ON: Dundurn Press, 1991.

992. Blake, Donald Edward. *Two Political Worlds: Parties and Voting in
     British Columbia*. Vancouver, BC: University of British Columbia
     Press, 1985.

993. Blum, Alan, and Peter McHugh. "The Risk of Theorizing and the
     Problem of the Good of Place: A Reformulation of Canadian
     Nationalism." 3, no. 3 (1978): 321-47.

994. Bowden, Gary. "Labor Unions in the Public Mind: The Canadian Case."
     Canadian Review of Sociology and Anthropology 26, no. 5 (1989):
     723-42.

995. Bozinoff, Lorne, and Peter MacIntosh. *60% Believe US Has Too Much
     Influence on Canada*. Toronto, ON: Gallup Canada, 1989.

996. Brown, Steven D. "In the Eye of the Beholder: Leader Images in
     Canada." *Canadian Journal of Political Science* 21, no. 4 (1988):
     729-55.

997. Burke, Mike et al. "Federal and Provincial Political Participation in Canada: Some Methodological and Substantive Considerations." *Canadian Review of Sociology and Anthropology* 15, no. 1 (1978): 61-75.

998. Burnham, Rebecca. "Youth Wing Flap: The NDP's Hold on Young Supporters May Be Slipping." *BC Report* 3, no. 5 (1991): 8-9.

999. Caldwell, Gary. "Discovering and Developing English-Canadian Nationalism in Quebec." *Canadian Review of Studies in Nationalism* 11, no. 2 (1984): 245-56.

1000. Came, Barry. "Opinions Unlike the Others: Quebecers Disclose Distinctive Attitudes." *Maclean's* 103, no. 1 (1990): cover, 18, 20.

1001. Canada. Task Force on Canadian Unity. *A Time To Speak: The Views of the Public*. Ottawa, ON: Minister of Supply and Services Canada, 1979.

1002. Canadian Council for International Cooperation. *Youth on Development; Survey of Opinions of Canadian Youth on International Aid and Development*. Ottawa, ON: The Council, 1971.

1003. Canadian Institute for International Peace and Security. *The 1990 CIIPS Public Opinion Survey: Changing Conceptions of Security: Public Attitudes in Canada*. Ottawa, ON: The Institute, 1990.

1004. Canadian Institute for International Peace and Security, and Harald Von Riekhoff. *Canadian Attitudes and Approaches to the United Nations Security Council*. Background Paper, 26. Ottawa, ON: The Institute, 1989.

1005. Canadian International Development Agency. *Report to CIDA: Public Attitudes toward International Development Assistance*. Hull, PQ: The Agency, 1988.

1006. Citizens' Forum on Canada's Future. *Citizens' Forum on Canada's Future: Report to the People and Government of Canada*. Ottawa, ON: Supply and Services Canada, 1991.

1007. Clarke, Harold D. et al. *Absent Mandate: Interpreting Change in Canadian Elections*. Toronto, ON: Gage Educational Pub. Co., 1991.

1008. Clarke, Harold D. et al. "Parliament and Political Support in Canada." *The American Political Science Review* 78 (1984): 452-69.

1009. Clarke, Harold D., and Allan Kornberg. "Evaluations and Evolution: Public Attitudes toward Canada's Federal Political Parties, 1965-1991." *Canadian Journal of Political Science* 26, no. 2 (1993): 287-311.

1010. Clarke, Harold D., and Allan Kornberg. "Moving Up the Political Escalator: Women Party Officials in the United States and Canada." *Journal of Politics* 41, no. 2 (1979): 442-77.

1011. Clarke, Harold D., and Richard G. Price. "A Note on the Pre-Nomination Role Socialization of Freshman Members of Parliament." *Canadian Journal of Political Science* 10, no. 2 (1977): 391-406.

1012. Corelli, Rae. "Border of Mirrors: Canadian Attitudes to America Are a Study in Sharp Contrasts." *Maclean's* 103, no. 1 (1990): cover, 37-38.

1013. Crowley, Terry. "New Canada Movement: Agrarian Youth Protest in the 1930s." *Ontario History* 80, no. 4 (1988): 311-25.

1014. Cullen, Dallas et al. "Anti-Americanism and Its Correlates." *Canadian Journal of Sociology* 3, no. 1 (1978): 103-20.

1015. Cullen, Dallas et al. "Towards the Development of a Canadian-American Scale: A Research Note." *Canadian Journal of Political Science* 11, no. 2 (1978): 409-18.

1016. Cuneo, Carl J., and James E. Curtis. "Quebec Separatism: An Analysis of Determinants within Social-Class Levels." *Canadian Review of Sociology and Anthropology* 11, no. 1 (1974): 1-29.

1017. Curtis, James E., and Ronald D. Lambert. "Educational Status and Reactions to Social and Political Heterogeneity." *Canadian Review of Sociology and Anthropology* 13, no. 2 (1976): 189-203.

1018. Delbridge, Clare. "Public Attitudes in Canada towards the United Nations." *Bulletin: United Nations Association in Canada* 12, no. 1 (1986): 2-5.

1019. Driedger, Leo. "Doctrinal Belief: A Major Factor in the Differential Perception of Social Issues." *Sociological Quarterly* 15, no. 1 (1974): 66-80.

1020. Driedger, Michael, Don Munton, and Canadian Institute for International Peace and Security. *Security, Arms Control and Defence: Public Attitudes in Canada - the 1989 CIIPS Public Opinion Survey*. Ottawa, ON: Canadian Institute for International Peace and Security, 1989.

1021. Ehrensaft, Philip, and Jennifer Beeman. "Leveraging the Farm Vote: The New Political Arithmetic of Agricultural Policy Formation." *The Canadian Journal of Agricultural Economics* 38, no. 4 (1990): 771-84.

1022. Evans, Paul Andrew. *Canadian Public Opinion on Relations with China: An Analysis of the Existing Survey Research*. Canada and the Pacific, Working Paper Series, no. 33. Downsview, ON: University of Toronto-York University, Joint Centre on Modern East Asia, 1985.

1023. Friedmann, Karl Anton. "The Public and the Ombudsman: Perceptions and Attitudes in Britain and in Alberta." *Canadian Journal of Political Science* 10 (September 1977): 497-525.

1024. Fulford, Robert. "Electioneering and the National Psyche." *Financial Times of Canada* 77, no. 14 (1988): 50.

1025. Gibbins, Roger. "Models of Nationalism: A Case Study of Political Ideologies in the Canadian West." *Canadian Journal of Political Science* 10, no. 2 (1977): 341-73.

1026. Gibbins, Roger, and Neil Nevitte. "Canadian Political Ideology: A Comparative Analysis." *Canadian Journal of Political Science* 18, no. 3 (1985): 577-98.

1027. Goldfarb Consultants Limited. *The Searching Nation: A Study of Canadians' Attitudes to the Future of Confederation: July, 1977*. Toronto, ON: Southam Press, 1977.

1028. Goldfarb, Martin. *Marching to a Different Drummer: An Essay on the Liberals and Conservatives in Convention*. Toronto, ON: Stoddart, 1988.

1029. Grabb, Edward G. *Canada and the United States: A Comparison of Selected Attitudes Concerning Social Control and Individual Liberties*. Edmonton Area Series Report, no. 11. Edmonton, AB: University of Alberta, Department of Sociology, Population Research Laboratory, 1979.

1030. Grabb, Edward G., and James E. Curtis. "English Canadian-American Differences in Orientation toward Social Control and Individual Rights." *Sociological Focus* 21, no. 2 (1988): 127-40.

1031. Grayson, J. Paul. "Plant Closures and Political Despair." *Canadian Review of Sociology and Anthropology* 23, no. 3 (1986): 331-49.

1032. Gregg, Allan, and Michael Posner. *The Big Picture: What Canadians Think about Almost Everything*. Toronto, ON: MacFarlane Walter & Ross, 1990.

1033. Harbour, Frances V. "Conscription and Socialization: Four Canadian Ministers." *Armed Forces and Society* 15, no. 2 (1989): 227-47.

1034. Head, Ivan L. "Ancient Attitudes Blind Us to Our Global Interdependence." *Canadian Speeches* 4, no. 10 (1991): 31-35.

1035. Heintzman, Ralph. "The Political Culture of Quebec, 1840-1960." *Political Attitudes and Behaviour* 16, no. 1 (1983): 3-59.

1036. Homel, David. "'Anglophobia': In the Wake of the Richler Controversy, Journalist William Johnson Puts Quebecois Society on the Couch (Anglophobie Made in Quebec)." *Quill and Quire* 58, no. 1 (1992): 14.

1037. Hoy, Claire. *Margin of Error: Pollsters and the Manipulation of Canadian Politics*. Toronto, ON: Key Porter Books, 1989.

1038. Johnston, William Atchison. "Social Class, Social Life and Political Attitudes in Canada." Ph.D. diss., York University, 1982.

1039. Johnston, William Atchison. "Social Divisions and Ideological Fragmentation." *Canadian Journal of Sociology* 12, no. 4 (1987): 315-29.

1040. Johnston, William Atchison, and Michael D. Ornstein. "Class, Work and Politics." *Canadian Review of Sociology and Anthropology* 19, no. 2 (1982): 196-214.

1041. Johnston, William Atchison, and Michael D. Ornstein. "Social Class and Political Ideology in Canada." *Canadian Review of Sociology and Anthropology* 22, no. 3 (1985): 369-93.

1042. Keddie, Vincent Gordon. "Class Identification and Party Preference among Manual Workers: The Influence of Community, Union Membership, and Kinship." *Canadian Review of Sociology and Anthropology* 17, no. 1 (1980): 24-36.

1043. Kielty, Frank, Clara Halton, and Peter Munsche. *Canadians Speak Out: The Canadian Gallup Polls.* Toronto, ON: McNamara Press, 1980.

1044. Kitchener (Ontario). Citizen-City Hall Communications Committee, and Sententia Inc. *Kitchener City Survey of Attitudes towards Local Government and Local Government Services, 1980.* Kitchener, ON: Citizen-City Hall Communications Committee, 1980.

1045. Kopinak, Kathryn. "Gender Differences in Political Ideology in Canada." *Canadian Review of Sociology and Anthropology* 24, no. 1 (1987): 23-38.

1046. Kornberg, Allan, and Keith Archer. "A Note on Quebec Attitudes toward Constitutional Options." *Law and Contemporary Problems* 45, no. 4 (1982): 71-85.

1047. Kuruvilla, Sarosh et al. "The Development of Members' Attitudes toward Their Unions: Sweden and Canada." *Industrial and Labor Relations Review* 46, no. 3 (1993): 499-514.

1048. Laczko, Leslie. "English Canadians and Quebecois Nationalism: An Empirical Analysis." *Canadian Review of Sociology and Anthropology* 15, no. 2 (1978): 206-17.

1049. Lambert, Ronald D. et al. "In Search of Left/Right Beliefs in the Canadian Electorate." *Canadian Journal of Political Science* 19, no. 3 (1986): 541-63.

1050. Lambert, Ronald D. "Question Design, Response Set and the Measurement of Left/Right Thinking in Survey Research." *Canadian Journal of Political Science* 16, no. 1 (1983): 135-44.

1051. Lambert, Ronald D. et al. "The Social Sources of Political Knowledge." *Canadian Journal of Political Science* 21, no. 2 (1988): 359-74.

1052. Lambert, Ronald D., and James E. Curtis. "Perceived Party Choice and Class Voting." *Canadian Journal of Political Science* 26, no. 2 (1993): 273-286.

1053. Lambert, Ronald D., and James E. Curtis. "Social Stratification and Canadians' Reactions to American Cultural Influences: Theoretical Problems." *International Journal of Comparative Sociology* 20, no. 3-4 (1979): 175-98.

1054. Langford, Tom. "Left/Right Orientation and Political Attitudes: A Reappraisal and Class Comparison." *Canadian Journal of Political Science* 24, no. 3 (1991): 475-98.

1055. Lanoue, David J. "Debates That Mattered: Voters' Reaction to the 1984 Canadian Leadership Debates." *Canadian Journal of Political Science* 24, no. 1 (1991): 51-65.

1056. LeDuc, Lawrence. "Canadian Attitudes towards Quebec Independence." *Public Opinion Quarterly* 41, no. 3 (1977): 347-55.

1057. LeDuc, Lawrence. "Partisan Change and Dealignment in Canada, Great Britain, and the United States." *Comparative Politics* 17 (July 1985): 379-98.

1058. LeDuc, Lawrence, and J. Alex Murray. "A Resurgence of Canadian Nationalism: Attitudes and Policy in the 1980's." In *Political Support in Canada: The Crisis Years*, edited by Allan Kornberg and Harold D. Clarke. Durham, NC: Duke University, 1982.

1059. Lucore, Robert E. "American Exceptionalism and the Economic Role of the Public Sector: Canada and the U.S. Compared." *International Journal of Social Economics* 16, no. 3 (1989): 34-43.

1060. MacDermid, R. H. "The Recall of Past Partisanship: Feeble Memories or Frail Concepts?" *Canadian Journal of Political Science* 22 (1989): 363-75.

1061. Macdonald, Helen Grace. *Canadian Public Opinion on the American Civil War*. Columbia Studies in the Social Sciences, no. 273. New York, NY: Octagon Books, 1974.

1062. Martinez, Michael D. "Intergenerational Transfer of Canadian Partisanships." *Canadian Journal of Political Science* 17, no. 1 (1984): 133-43.

1063. McKague, Ormond. "The Saskatchewan CCF: Education Policy and the Rejection of Socialism, 1942-1948." *Journal of Educational Thought* 14, no. 2 (1980): 138-59.

1064. McKee, Janet. "Effect of Domestic Labour and Gender on the Relationship between Class and Political Attitudes." *Atlantis* 14, no. 2 (1989): 63-71.

1065. Meisel, John. *Cleavages, Parties and Values in Canada*. Sage Professional Papers in Contemporary Political Sociology, ser. no. 06-003. London, ON: Sage Publications, 1974.

1066. Menzies, Heather. *The Railroad's Not Enough: Canada Now.* Toronto, ON: Clarke, Irwin, 1978.

1067. Monroe, Kristen. "The Economy and Political Support: The Canadian Case." *The Journal of Politics* 48 (1986): 616-47.

1068. Moore, Gwen, and Glenna D. Spitze. *Women and Politics: Activism, Attitudes and Office-Holding.* Research in Politics and Society, no. 2. Greenwich, CT: JAI Press, 1986.

1069. Morris, Raymond N. "Canada as a Family: Ontario Responses to the Quebec Independence Movement." *Canadian Review of Sociology and Anthropology* 21, no. 2 (1984): 181-201.

1070. Munton, Don. *The 1990 CIIPS Public Opinion Survey: Changing Conceptions of Security: Public Attitudes in Canada.* Ottawa, ON: Canadian Institute for International Peace and Security, 1990.

1071. Munton, Don, and Michael Slack. "Canadian Attitudes on Disarmament." *International Perspectives* (July/August 1982): 9-12.

1072. Nadeau, Richard, and Andre Blais. "Do Canadians Distinguish between Parties? Perceptions of Party Competence." *Canadian Journal of Political Science* 23, no. 2 (1990): 317-33.

1073. Nevitte, Neil et al. "The Ideological Contours of 'New Politics' in Canada: Policy, Mobilization and Partisan Support." *Canadian Journal of Political Science* 22 (1989): 475-503.

1074. Nielsen, Sharon Froese, and Patricia Froese. "Regional Variation in Attitudes toward the Peace Movement and Nuclear Disarmament." *Canadian Woman Studies* 9, no. 1 (1988): 90-91.

1075. Ogmundson, Richard Lewis. "A Note on the Ambiguous Meanings of Survey Research Measures Which Use the Words 'Left' and 'Right'." *Canadian Journal of Political Science* 12, no. 4 (1979): 799-805.

1076. Ogmundson, Richard Lewis. "On the Use of Party Image Variables to Measure the Political Distinctiveness of a Class Vote: The Canadian Case." *Canadian Journal of Sociology* 1, no. 2 (1975): 169-77.

1077. Ornstein, Michael D. *Political Cleavages in the Canadian Capitalist Class.* Downsview, ON: York University, Institute for Behavioural Research, 1981.

1078. Ornstein, Michael D., and H. Michael Stevenson. "Elite and Public
      Opinion before the Quebec Referendum: A Commentary on the
      State in Canada." *Canadian Journal of Political Science* 14, no. 4
      (1981): 745-74.

1079. Palmer, W. H. et al. *Public Attitude Survey - Waterloo Region Review
      Commission; Analysis of Public Attitudes and Perceptions of Local
      Government in the Region of Waterloo, Ontario.* Toronto, ON:
      Micromedia, 1978.

1080. Penner, Norman. "The Socialist Idea in Canadian Political Thought."
      Ph.D. diss., University of Toronto, 1975.

1081. Petrie, Brian M. "Examination of a Stereotype: Athletes as
      Conservatives." *International Review of Sport Sociology* 12, no. 3
      (1977): 51-62.

1082. Pratt, Geraldine. "Class, Home, and Politics." *Canadian Review of
      Sociology and Anthropology* 24, no. 1 (1987): 39-57.

1083. Preece, Rod. "The Myth of the Red Tory." *Canadian Journal of Political
      and Social Theory* 1, no. 2 (1977): 3-28.

1084. Presthus, Robert, and William V. Monopoli. "Bureaucracy in the
      United States and Canada: Social, Attitudinal and Behavioral
      Variables." *International Journal of Comparative Sociology* 18, no.
      1-2 (1977): 176-90.

1085. Redekop, John Harold, ed. *The Star-Spangled Beaver.* Toronto, ON:
      Peter Martin Associates, 1971.

1086. Resnick, Philip. "Letter to a Quebecois Friend: Tory Support in Quebec
      Gave the Mulroney Government the Majority It Needed to Carry
      Out Its Plans for the Free Trade Agreement." *The Canadian
      Forum* 68, no. 781 (1989): 16-18.

1087. Richert, Jean Pierre. "Political Socialization in Quebec: Young People's
      Attitudes toward Government." *Canadian Journal of Political
      Science* 6, no. 2 (1973): 303-13.

1088. Ross, David J. "Official Canadian Attitudes towards the
      Commonwealth." *Australian Journal of Politics and History* 26, no.
      2 (1980): 183-92.

1089. Rutherford, Paul Frederic William. "The New Nationality, 1864-1897:
      A Study of the National Aims and Ideas of English Canada in the
      Late Nineteenth-Century." Ph.D. diss., University of Toronto,
      1973.

1090. Schell, Bernadette H., and Andrew Loeb. "An Investigation of General Happiness Level, Collective Bargaining Attitudes, Job Satisfaction, and University and Union Commitment of Faculty Members in Canada." *Journal of Social Behavior and Personality* 1, no. 4 (1986): 537-56.

1091. Schmid, Carol L. "Quebec in the 1970s-1980s: Submerged Nation or Canadian Fringe?" *Research in Political Sociology* 2 (1986): 269-91.

1092. Sigelman, Lee, and William G. Vanderbok. "Legislators, Bureaucrats, and Canadian Democracy: The Long and the Short of It." *Canadian Journal of Political Science* 10, no. 3 (1977): 615-23.

1093. Silver, Arthur Isaac. *The French-Canadian Idea of Confederation, 1864-1900*. Toronto, ON: University of Toronto Press, 1982.

1094. Silver, Arthur Isaac. "Ontario's Alleged Fanaticism in the Riel Affair." *Canadian Historical Review* 69 (1988): 21-50.

1095. Skogstad, Grace. "Agrarian Protest in Alberta." *Canadian Review of Sociology and Anthropology* 17, no. 1 (1980): 55-73.

1096. Sorrentino, Richard M. *Opinion Change in a Crisis: Effects of the 1970 Canadian Kidnapping Crisis on Political and Ethnic Attitudes.* Research Bulletin, no. 258. London, ON: University of Western Ontario, Department of Psychology, 1973.

1097. Sorrentino, Richard M., and Neil Vidmar. "Impact of Events: Short vs Long-Term Effects of a Crisis." *Public Opinion Quarterly* 38, no. 2 (1974): 271-79.

1098. Steggart, Frank X., and Janet M. Howell. *Citizen Views in Greater Halifax: Attitudes toward Municipal Services, Public Education and Governmental Performance*. Halifax, NS: Metropolitan Area Planning Committee, 1972.

1099. Stewart, Walter. *Divide and Con; Canadian Politics at Work*. Toronto, ON: New Press, 1973.

1100. Stothart, Paul. "Exploring Alberta Myths: Albertans Hate Government, Right? . . . Love Competitive Free Enterprise, Right? . . . Are Under-represented in Ottawa. Try Again." *Policy Options Politiques* 9, no. 9 (1988): 3-7.

1101. Suleiman, Michael W. "Development of Public Opinion on the Palestine Question." *Journal of Palestine Studies* 13, no. 3 (51) (1984): 87-116.

1102. Ullman, Stephen H. "Political Disaffection in the Province of New Brunswick: Manifestations and Sources." *American Review of Canadian Studies* 20, no. 2 (1990): 151-77.

1103. Von Riekhoff, Harald, and Canadian Institute for International Peace and Security. *Canadian Attitudes and Approaches to the United Nations Security Council.* Background Paper, no. 26. Ottawa, ON: Canadian Institute for International Peace and Security, 1989.

1104. Weinfeld, Morton et al. "The Effect of the Holocaust on Selected Socio-Political Attitudes of Adult Children of Survivors." *Canadian Review of Sociology and Anthropology* 23, no. 3 (1986): 365-82.

1105. Weiss, Alan Z. "Canadian and East German Attitudes towards War and Peace (Canadian Institute of International Peace and Security Questionnaire)." *Peace Research* 21, no. 4 (1989): 17-26+.

1106. Williams, A. Paul. "Social Origins and Elite Politics in Canada: The Impact of Background Differences on Attitudes toward the Welfare State." *Canadian Journal of Sociology* 14, no. 1 (1989): 67-87.

1107. Wilson, John. "The Canadian Political Cultures: Towards a Redefinition of the Nature of the Canadian Political System." *Canadian Journal of Political Science* 7, no. 3 (1974): 438-83.

1108. Winn, Conrad, and James Twiss. "The Spatial Analysis of Political Cleavages and the Case of the Ontario Legislature." *Canadian Journal of Political Science* 10, no. 2 (1977): 287-310.

1109. Wise, Sydney F., and Robert Craig Brown. *Canada Views the United States: Nineteenth-Century Political Attitudes.* Toronto, ON: Macmillan of Canada, 1972.

1110. Yelaya, Shankar A. "Gray Power: Agenda for Future Research." *Canadian Journal on Aging* 8, no. 2 (1989): 118-27.

1111. Zipp, John F., and Joel Smith. "The Structure of Electoral Political Participation." *American Journal of Sociology* 85, no. 1 (1979): 167-77.

1112. Zubrzychi, Jack. *Canadian Public Opinion and Government Policy toward the Middle East.* Occasional Paper. Kingston, ON: Near East Cultural and Educational Foundation of Canada, 1986.

Section 9

Native Canadians

1113. Anderson, Karen. "As Gentle As Little Lambs: Images of Huron and Montagnais-Naskapi Women in the Writings of the 17th Century Jesuits." *Canadian Review of Sociology and Anthropology* 25, no. 4 (1988): 560-76.

1114. Boldt, Menno. "Enlightenment Values, Romanticism, and Attitudes toward Political Status: A Study of Native Leaders in Canada." *Canadian Review of Sociology and Anthropology* 18, no. 4 (1981): 545-65.

1115. Boldt, Menno. "Indian Leaders in Canada: Attitudes toward Extralegal Activities." *Journal of Ethnic Studies* 8, no. 1 (1980): 71-83.

1116. Boldt, Menno. "Philosophy, Politics and Extralegal Action: Native Indian Leaders in Canada." *Ethnic and Racial Studies* 4, no. 2 (1981): 205-21.

1117. Braroe, Niels Winther. *Indian and White: Self-Image and Interaction in a Canadian Plains Community*. Stanford, CA: Stanford University Press, 1975.

1118. Canada. Department of Indian Affairs and Northern Development. Indian and Inuit Affairs Program. *Overview of Some Recent Research on Attitudes in Canada toward Indian People*. Ottawa, ON: Indian and Northern Affairs Canada, 1983.

1119. Canada. Indian and Inuit Affairs Program. *Preliminary Survey of Trends in Non-Native Attitudes towards Indian People*. Ottawa, ON: Canada Department of Indian Affairs and Northern Development, Indian and Inuit Affairs Program, Research Branch, 1977.

1120. Canada. Research Branch. Policy Research and Evaluation. Indian and Inuit Affairs Program. *An Overview of Some Recent Research on Attitudes in Canada towards Indian People*. Ottawa, ON: Indian and Northern Affairs Program, 1983.

1121. Carasco, Emily F. "Canadian Native Children: Have Child Welfare Laws Broken the Circle?" *Canadian Journal of Family Law* 5, no. 1 (1986): 111-38.

1122. Clifton, Rodney A. "Research Notes --Self-Concept and Attitudes: A Comparison of Canadian Indian and Non-Indian Students." *Canadian Review of Sociology and Anthropology* 12, no. 4 (1975): 577-84.

1123. Coldevin, Gary O. "Some Effects of Frontier Television in a Canadian Eskimo Community." *Journalism Quarterly* 53, no. 1 (1976): 34-39.

1124. Dunn, Christopher. *Canadian Political Debates: Opposing Views on Issues that Divide Canadians.* Toronto: McClelland and Stewart, 1995.

1125. Flanagan, Thomas, and Nicholas Griffin. "The Agricultural Argument and Original Appropriation: Indian Lands and Political Philosophy." *Canadian Journal of Political Science* 22, no. 3 (1989): 589-602.

1126. Gibbins, Roger, and J. Rick Ponting. *Canadians' Opinions and Attitudes towards Indians and Indian Issues: Findings of a National Study.* Ottawa, ON: Indian and Northern Affairs Canada, 1978.

1127. Glellner, Barbara M. "A Matched-Group Comparison of Drug Use and Problem Behavior among Canadian Indian and White Adolescents." *Journal of Early Adolescence* 14, no. 1 (1994): 24-48.

1128. Haddock, Geoffrey et al. "The (Limited) Role of Trait-Laden Stereotypes in Predicting Attitudes toward Native Peoples." *British Journal of Social Psychology* 33, no. 1 (1994): 83-106.

1129. Harding, Jim et al. *Overcoming Systemic Discrimination against Aboriginal People in Saskatchewan: Brief to the Indian Justice Review Committee and the Metis Justice Review Committee, November 1991.* Regina, SK: University of Regina, School of Human Justice, Prairie Justice Research, 1992.

1130. Hobart, Charles W. "Industrial Employment of Rural Indigenes: The Case of Canada." *Human Organization* 41, no. 1 (1982): 54-63.

1131. Hodgson, Corinne. "The Social and Political Implications of Tuberculosis among Native Canadians." *Canadian Review of Sociology and Anthropology* 19, no. 4 (1982): 502-12.

1132. Hultkrantz, A'ke. "The Hare Indians: Notes on Their Traditional Culture and Religion, Past and Present." *Ethnos* 38, no. 1-4 (1973): 113-52.

1133. Hylton, John H. "Locking Up Indians in Saskatchewan: Some Recent Findings." *Canadian Ethnic Studies* 13, no. 3 (1981): 144-51.

1134. Indian-Eskimo Association of Canada. *The Attitudes of Toronto Students towards the Canadian Indians*. Toronto, ON: The Association, 1971.

1135. Jarvenpa, Robert. "The Political Economy and Political Ethnicity of American Indian Adaptations and Identities." *Ethnic and Racial Studies* 8, no. 1 (1985): 29-48.

1136. Jilek, Wolfgang G., and Chunilal Roy. "Homicide Committed by Canadian Indians and Non-Indians." *International Journal of Offender Therapy and Comparative Criminology* 20, no. 3 (1976): 201-16.

1137. Keeslng-Soonias, Beverly. "Hope Grows in Native Communities." *Catholic New Times* 15, no. 13 (1991): 1, 17.

1138. Maracle, Brian. "Natives Are People, Too." *Content* (July-August 1991): 19.

1139. McDermott, J. R. "Attitudes toward Indians: Effect of Measurement Technique, Proximity, and Perceived Attitude Similarity." Master's thesis, University of Guelph, 1974.

1140. McPhie, Judith Lynn, and Jane Beynon. "Attitude Change through Cultural Immersion: A Grade Four Enrichment Curriculum." *Canadian Ethnic Studies* 21, no. 1 (1989): 65-76.

1141. Nagler, Mark. "A Sociological Overview of Canadian Indians." *Journal of Comparative Sociology* 2 (1974): 102-13.

1142. Peters, E. et al. *The Ontario Métis: Characteristics and Identity*. Native Issues, 4. Winnipeg, MB: University of Winnipeg, Institute of Urban Studies, 1991.

1143. Philip, D. P. (David Paul). "Attitudes to Resource Development among Native People in Northern Ontario." Master's thesis, University of Guelph, 1980.

1144. Ponting, J. Rick. "Conflict and Change in Indian/Non-Indian Relations in Canada: Comparison of 1976 and 1979 National Attitude Surveys." *Canadian Journal of Sociology* 9, no. 2 (1984): 137-58.

1145. Ponting, J. Rick. "Public Opinion on Aboriginal Peoples Issues in Canada." *Canadian Social Trends* 11 (1988): 9-17.

1146. Québec (Province). Secrétariat aux affaires autochtones. *Opinions of and Attitudes towards Aboriginal People: A Survey of Quebecers.* Montreal, PQ: Gouvernement du Québec, Ministère du Conseil exécutif, Secrétariat aux affaires autochtones, 1991.

1147. Ridington, Robin. "Technology, World View, and Adaptive Strategy in a Northern Hunting Society." *Canadian Review of Sociology and Anthropology* 19, no. 4 (1982): 469-81.

1148. Sokoloski, Elizabeth H. "Canadian First Nations Women's Beliefs about Pregnancy and Parental Care." *Canadian Journal of Nursing Research* 27, no. 1 (1995): 89-100.

1149. Stevenson, Ian. "The Belief and Cases Related to Reincarnation among the Haida." *Journal of Anthropological Research* 31, no. 4 (1975): 364-75.

1150. Stymeist, David H. *Ethnics and Indians: Social Relations in a Northwestern Ontario Town.* Toronto, ON: Peter Martin Associates, 1975.

1151. Taylor, Donald M., and Stephen C. Wright. "Language Attitudes in a Multilingual Northern Community." *Canadian Journal of Native Studies* 9, no. 1 (1989): 85-119.

1152. Trask, Noah Albert. "Attitudes, Social-Economic Status and Achievement of Inuit Students in Labrador." M. Ed. thesis, Memorial University of Newfoundland, 1979.

1153. Wright, D., and Canada. Library of Parliament. Research Branch. *Indian Self-Government.* Current Issue Review, 86-31E. Ottawa, ON: Library of Parliament, Research Branch, 1987.

Section 10

Gender and Sexuality Behaviour

1154. Abernathy, Thomas J. "A Test of Hypotheses Concerning Canadian Adolescents' Attitudes about Female Employment." *International Journal of Sociology of the Family* 8, no. 1 (1978): 69-80.

1155. Alberta. Premier's Council on Science and Technology. *Women in Science and Technology*. Edmonton, AB: The Council, 1992.

1156. Alberta Women's Secretariat. *Person to Person: An Alberta Dialogue on Economic Equity for Women*. Edmonton, AB: The Secretariat, 1989.

1157. Aube, Jennifer, and Richard Koestner. "Gender Characteristics and Relationship Adjustment: Another Look at Similarity-Complementarity Hypotheses." *Journal of Personality* 63, no. 4 (1995): 879-904.

1158. Baker, Maureen. *What Will Tomorrow Bring?: A Study of the Aspirations of Adolescent Women*. Ottawa, ON: Canadian Advisory Council on the Status of Women, 1985.

1159. Bardis, Panos D. "The Pill in Various Countries." *International Review of Sociology* 18, no. 1-3 (1982): 128-35.

1160. Baxter, Janeen, and Emily W. Kane. "Dependence and Independence: A Cross-National Analysis of Gender Inequality and Gender Attitudes." *Gender and Society* 9, no. 2 (1995): 193-215.

1161. Beaman, Arthur L. et al. "A Direct Test of and an Alternative Explanation for Judgments of Attractiveness of Supporters of the Women's Movement." *Canadian Journal of Behavioural Science* 16, no. 3 (1984): 191-95.

1162. Beer, Frances. "The Continuity of Female Stereotypes: From Recluse to Bunny: (Reprint)." *Canadian Woman Studies* 11, no. 3 (1991): 77-79.

1163. Berger, Esther M. "Why Women Fear Money." *Newsweek* 115, no. 11 (1990): 10.

1164. Bibby, Reginald Wayne. "The Moral Mosaic: Sexuality in the Canadian 80s." *Social Indicators Research* 2 (August 1983): 171-84.

1165. Bielay, George, and Edward S. Herold. "Popular Magazines as a Source of Sexual Information for University Women." *Canadian Journal of Human Sexuality* 4, no. 4 (1995): 247-62.

1166. Billson, Janet Mancini. "Keepers of the Culture: Attitudes toward Women's Liberation and the Women's Movement in Canada." *Women and Politics* 14, no. 1 (1994): 1.

1167. Bowd, Alan D., and Cynthia H. Loos. "Gender Differences in Adoption of AIDS Preventive Behaviors: Implications for Women's AIDS Education Programs." *Women's Health Issues* 5, no. 1 (1995): 21-26.

1168. Boyd, Monica. *Canadian Attitudes toward Women: Thirty Years of Change - 1954-1984.; Attitudes des Canadiens a l'egard des femmes*. Ottawa, ON: Labour Canada, 1984.

1169. Boyd, Monica. "English-Canadian and French-Canadian Attitudes toward Women: Results of the Canadian Gallup Polls." *Journal of Comparative Family Studies* 6, no. 2 (1975): 153-69.

1170. Brock, Debi. "Prostitutes Are Scapegoats in the AIDS Panic." *Resources for Feminist Research* 18, no. 2 (1989): 13-17.

1171. Brown, Lil. "Is There Sexual Freedom for Our Aging Population in Long-Term Care Institutions? " *Journal of Gerontological Social Work* 13, no. 3-4 (1989): 75-93.

1172. Burt, Sandra. "Canadian Women's Groups in the 1980s: Organizational Development and Policy Influence." *Canadian Public Policy* 16 (March 1990): 17-28.

1173. Canada. Department of National Health and Welfare. Policy Research and Long Range Planning Branch. *Changing Dependence of Women: Roles, Beliefs and Inequality*. Social Security Research Reports, 5. Ottawa, ON: The Branch, 1978.

1174. Clark, Peter, and Anthony Davis. "The Power of Dirt: An Exploration of Secular Defilement in Anglo-Canadian Culture." *Canadian Review of Sociology and Anthropology* 26, no. 4 (1989): 650-73.

1175. Cohen, Leah. *Small Expectations: Society's Betrayal of Older Women*. Toronto, ON: McClelland and Stewart, 1984.

1176. Consultation Group on Employment Equity for Women (Canada). *Gender Balance: More Than the Numbers: Report*. [Ottawa], ON: Treasury Board, 1992.

1177. Consultation Group on Employment Equity for Women (Canada). *Looking to the Future: Challenging the Attitudinal and Cultural Barriers to Women in the Public Services*. Ottawa, ON: Treasury Board of Canada, Secretariat, Planning and Communications Directorate, 1995.

1178. Data Laboratories Research Consultants. *Report of a Survey of the Attitudes of Canadians toward the Women's Rights Movement and the Role of Women in Society*. Montreal, PQ: Data Laboratories Research Consultants, 1979.

1179. Davies, Scott. "Reproduction and Resistance in Canadian High Schools: An Empirical Examination of the Willis Thesis." *British Journal of Sociology* 46, no. 4 (1995): 662-87.

1180. Davis, Dona Lee. "Newfoundland Change of Life: Insights into the Medicalization of Menopause." *Journal of Cross-Cultural Gerontology* 4, no. 1 (1989): 49-73.

1181. Day, D. *Young Women in Nova Scotia: A Study of Attitudes, Behaviour and Aspirations*. Halifax, NS: Nova Scotia Advisory Council on the Status of Women, 1990.

1182. Dion, Kenneth L., and Regina A. Schuller. "Ms. Stereotype: Its Generality and Its Relation to Managerial and Marital Status Stereotypes." *The Canadian Journal of Behavioural Science* 23, no. 1 (1991): 25-40.

1183. Dionne, Michelle et al. "Feminist Ideology as a Predictor of Body Dissatisfaction in Women." *Sex Roles* 33, no. 3-4 (1995): 277-87.

1184. Dobrowolsky, Sonia A. "A Study of Women in Social Work: Their Aspirations to Administrative Positions and Attitudes toward Discrimination." M.S.W. thesis, University of Windsor, 1975.

1185. Dulude, L., and Elise Rosen. *Women and Aging: A Report on the Rest of Our Lives*. Ottawa, ON: Canadian Advisory Council on the Status of Women, 1978.

1186. Dunsmuir, M. *Abortion: Constitutional and Legal Developments*. Rev ed. Current Issue Review, 89-10E. Ottawa, ON: Library of Parliament, Research Branch, 1991.

1187. El Gamal, Heather. "Social Support, Self-Esteem, and
        Pregnancy-Related Attitudes among Pregnant Adolescents." M.Ed.
        thesis, University of Manitoba, 1987.

1188. Ellis, Diana. "Grounding Our Beliefs on Women and the Economy."
        Women's Education 6, no. 4 (1988): 9-11.

1189. Etkin, Mark. "Ending the Brutality: The Men's Movement." *Canadian
        Dimension* 25, no. 1 (1991): 35-37.

1190. Friel, James K. et al. "Effect of a Promotion Campaign on Attitudes of
        Adolescent Females towards Breastfeeding." *Canadian Journal of
        Public Health* 80, no. 3 (1989): 195-99.

1191. Gee, Ellen M. "Preferred Timing of Women's Life Events: A Canadian
        Study." *International Journal of Aging and Human Development*
        31, no. 4 (1990): 279-94.

1192. George, Theresa. "Canadian Sikh Women and Menopause: A Different
        View." *International Journal of Sociology of the Family* 18, no. 2
        (1988): 297-307.

1193. Gibbins, Roger et al. "Attitudes and Ideology: Correlates of Liberal
        Attitudes towards the Role of Women." *Journal of Comparative
        Family Studies* 9, no. 1 (1978): 19-40.

1194. Giroux, Carolyn Joan. "Correlates of Attitudes towards Women in
        Management and Employment Equity Programs for Women in the
        Public Service." Ph.D. diss., Carleton University, 1995.

1195. Goh, Swee C., and Laird W. Mealiea. "Fear of Success and Its
        Relationship to the Job Performance, Tenure, and Desired Job
        Outcomes of Women." *Canadian Journal of Behavioural Science*
        16, no. 1 (1984): 65-75.

1196. Gold, Dolores, and David Andres. "Relations between Maternal
        Employment and Development of Nursery School Children."
        Canadian Journal of Behavioural Science 10, no. 2 (1978): 116-29.

1197. Grindstaff, Carl F. *The Pharmacist and Family Planning: New Roles
        and Responsibilities.* North Quincy, MA: Christopher Publishing
        House, 1980.

1198. Hall, David Ray. "Marriage as a Pure Relationship: Exploring the Link
        between Premarital Cohabitation and Divorce in Canada." *Journal
        of Comparative Family Studies* 27, no. 1 (1996): 1-12.

1199. Hartnagel, Timothy F. *Feminism and Religious Behaviour: Greeley Revisited in Western Canada.* Edmonton Area Series Report, no. 71. Edmonton, AB: University of Alberta, Department of Sociology, Population Research Laboratory, 1990.

1200. Hartnagel, Timothy F. "Public Opinion and the Legalization of Abortion." *Canadian Review of Sociology and Anthropology* 22, no. 3 (1985): 411-30.

1201. Herold, Edward S., and Marilyn Shirley Goodwin. "Adamant Virgins, Potential Nonvirgins and Nonvirgins." *Journal of Sex Research* 17, no. 2 (1981): 97-113.

1202. Herold, Edward S., and Marilyn Shirley Goodwin. "Premarital Sexual Guilt." *Canadian Journal of Behavioural Science* 13, no. 1 (1981): 65-75.

1203. Herold, Edward S., and Marilyn Shirley Goodwin. "Premarital Sexual Guilt and Contraceptive Attitudes and Behavior." *Family Relations* 30, no. 2 (1981): 247-53.

1204. Herold, Edward S., and Lynne M. Samson. "Differences between Women Who Begin Pill Use Before and After First Intercourse: Ontario, Canada." *Family Planning Perspectives* 12, no. 6 (1980): 304- 5.

1205. Heyward, Carter, and Suzanne R. Hiatt. "The Churches Ponder Evermore: The Trivialization of Women." *Christianity and Crisis* 38, no. 10 (1978): 158-62.

1206. Hilton, N. Zoe. "When Is an Assault Not an Assault? The Canadian Public's Attitudes towards Wife and Stranger Assault." *Journal of Family Violence* 4, no. 4 (1989): 323-37.

1207. Hinch, Ronald. "Canada's New Sexual Assault Laws: A Step Forward for Women?" *Contemporary Crisis* 9, no. 1 (1985): 33-44.

1208. Hobart, Charles W. "Changing Profession and Practice of Sexual Standards: A Study of Young Anglophone and Francophone Canadians." *Journal of Comparative Family Studies* 15, no. 2 (1984): 231- 55.

1209. Holman, Roy Paul. "The Perceived Status of Female Athletes by Male and Female Athletes and Non-Athletes in Canada and the United States." Ed.D. dissertation, University of North Carolina at Greensboro, 1978.

1210. Hornick, Joseph Phillip. "Premarital Sexual Attitudes and Behavior."
      Sociological Quarterly 19, no. 4 (1978): 534-44.

1211. Hornick, Joseph Phillip. "Premarital Sexual Attitudes and Behaviour:
      A Reference Group Contingent-Factor Theory." Ph.D. diss.,
      University of Waterloo, 1975.

1212. Johnson, Ronald W. et al. "Perceived Attractiveness as a Function of
      Support for the Feminist Movement: Not Necessarily a Put-Down
      of Women." *Canadian Journal of Behavioural Science* 10, no. 3
      (1978): 214-21.

1213. Joint Conference of Ministers Responsible for the Status of Women and
      Labour Market Matters. *Training Women in the Workplace:
      Federal, Provincial, Territorial Ministers Meeting.* Halifax, NS:
      Ministry of Skills Development, 1987.

1214. Kitchen, D. A. (Dorothy Anne). "Contraceptive Attitudes and Behaviour
      of Young Single Males." M.Sc. thesis, University of Guelph, 1983.

1215. Lam, Selina Yee-Kay. "The Social Determinants of Abortion Attitudes:
      A Sample of Edmonton Females." Master's thesis, University of
      Manitoba, 1990.

1216. Lawrence, K. G. et al. "Women's Attitudes toward and Experience with
      Sexually Explicit Materials." *The Journal of Sex Research* 24
      (1988): 161-69.

1217. Lazar, Morty M. "The Role of Women in Synagogue Ritual in Canadian
      Conservative Congregations." *Jewish Journal of Sociology* 20, no. 2
      (1978): 165-71.

1218. MacDougall, J. C., and Morin S. "Sexual Attitudes and Self-Reported
      Behavior of Congenitally Disabled Adults." *Canadian Journal of
      Behavioural Science* 11, no. 3 (1979): 189-204.

1219. MacRae, Hazel. "Older Women and Identity Maintenance in Later
      Life." *Canadian Journal on Aging* 9, no. 3 (1990): 248-67.

1220. Manion, Eileen. "We Objects Object: Pornography and the Women's
      Movement." *Canadian Journal of Political and Social Theory* 15,
      no. 1-3 (1991): 285-300.

1221. Manley-Casimir, Michael E., and Downey, (L. W.) Research Associates.
      *Public Attitudes toward Illegitimacy in Alberta: A Report to
      Alberta Health and Social Development.* Edmonton, AB: Alberta
      Department of Health and Social Development, 1973.

1222. Marsman, Joan C., and Edward S. Herold. "Attitudes toward Sex Education and Values in Sex Education." *Family Relations* 35 (1986): 357-61.

1223. Maupin, Helen E., and Ronald J. Fisher. "The Effects of Superior Female Performance and Sex-Role Orientation on Gender Conformity." *Canadian Journal of Behavioural Science* 21, no. 1 (1989): 55-69.

1224. McDonald, Gary J., and Robert J. Moore. "Sex-Role Self-Concepts of Homosexual Men and Their Attitudes toward Both Women and Male Homosexuality." *Journal of Homosexuality* 4, no. 1 (1978): 3-14.

1225. Miall, Charlene E. "Reproductive Technology vs. the Stigma of Involuntary Childlessness." *Social Casework* 70 (1989): 43-50.

1226. Michalski, Andrzej B. "Essex County Social Workers: Their Attitudes toward Women." M.S.W. thesis, University of Windsor, 1976.

1227. Miles, Angela. "Feminist Radicalism in the 1980's." *Canadian Journal of Political and Social Theory* 9, no. 1-2 (1985): 16-39.

1228. Myers, Michael F. "The Professional Woman as Patient: A Review and an Appeal." *Canadian Journal of Psychiatry* 27, no. 3 (1982): 236-40.

1229. Nett, Emily M. "An Ecological Analysis of Urban Therapeutic Abortion Rates." *Social Biology* 25, no. 3 (1978): 235-42.

1230. Osborn, R. W., and B. Silkey. "Husbands' Attitudes towards Abortion and Canadian Abortion Law." *Journal of Biosocial Science* 12, no. 1 (1980): 21-30.

1231. Peat, Marwick and Partners. *National Population Study of Prostitution and Pornography*. Working Papers on Pornography and Prostitution, Report no. 6. Ottawa, ON: Department of Justice, Policy, Programs and Research Branch, Research and Statistics Section, 1984.

1232. Pennell, Joan Thrush. "Consensual Bargaining: Labor Negotiations in Battered-Women's Programs." *Journal of Progressive Human Services* 1, no. 1 (1990): 59-74.

1233. Prince Edward Island. Advisory Council on the Status of Women. *Diversity, Vitality and Change: 1985/88*. Charlottetown, PE: The Council, 1988.

1234. Proulx, Monique Cecile. "Personal, Family and Institutional Factors Associated with Attitudes toward Women's Roles among French-Canadian College Students." Ph.D. diss., Michigan State University, 1976.

1235. Rayside, David, and Scott Bowler. "Public Opinion and Gay Rights." *Canadian Review of Sociology and Anthropology* 25, no. 4 (1988): 649-60.

1236. Redmond, Marcia A. "Attitudes of Adolescent Males toward Adolescent Pregnancy and Fatherhood." *Family Relations* 34, no. 3 (1985): 337-42.

1237. Rice, Carla, and Leslie Langdon. "Women's Struggles with Food and Weight As Survival Strategies." *Canadian Woman Studies* 12, no. 1 (1991): 30-33.

1238. Ross, Aileen D. "Some Comments on the Home Roles of Businesswomen in India, Australia, and Canada." *Journal of Comparative Family Studies* 8, no. 3 (1977): 327-40.

1239. Rowland, Robyn. "Women Who Do and Women Who Don't, Join the Women's Movement: Issues for Conflict and Collaboration." *Sex Roles* 14, no. 11-12 (1986): 679-92.

1240. Russell, Margaret Leora, and Edgar J. Love. "Contraceptive Prescription: Physician Beliefs, Attitudes and Socio-demographic Characteristics." *Canadian Journal of Public Health* 82, no. 4 (1991): 259-63.

1241. Ryan, Beth. "Young Women Holding on to a Fairy-Tale View of the World." *Atlantic* 11, no. 2 (1989): 11.

1242. Saskatchewan Consumer and Corporate Affairs. *Pornography: A Guide to Community and Family Education.* Regina, SK: Saskatchewan Consumer and Corporate Affairs, 1988.

1243. Schmid, Carol. "The Changing Status of Women in the United States and Canada: An Overview." *Sociological Symposium* 15 (Spring 1976): 1-27.

1244. Seidler, Vic. "Redefining Masculinity: Excerpt from the New Sexuality." *Canadian Dimension* 25, no. 8 (1991): 33-36.

1245. Shorter, Edward. "On Writing the History of Rape." *Signs* 3, no. 2 (1977): 471-82.

1246. Souza, Margaret de. "Colours of Menopause." *Healthsharing* 11, no. 4 (1990): 14-17.

1247. Sutherland, Sharon L. "The Unambitious Female: Women's Low Professional Aspirations." *Signs* 3, no. 4 (1978): 774-94.

1248. Theobald, William F., and D. Doherty. *Female in Public Recreation - A Study of Participation and Administrative Attitudes.* Toronto, ON: Ontario Ministry of Culture and Recreation, Sports and Fitness Division, 1976.

1249. Thomas, B. Helen, and Ellen Jamieson. "Childhood Sexuality Transmitted Diseases and Child Sexual Abuse: Results of a Canadian Survey of Three Professional Groups." *Child Abuse and Neglect* 19, no. 9 (1995): 1019-29.

1250. Tietjen, Anne Marie, and Christine F. Bradley. "Social Support and Maternal Psychosocial Adjustment during the Transition to Parenthood." *Canadian Journal of Behavioural Science* 17, no. 2 (1985): 109-21.

1251. Timberger, Rosemary, and Michael J. MacLean. "Maternal Employment: The Child's Perspective." *Journal of Marriage and the Family* 44, no. 2 (1982): 469-75.

1252. Trute, B. *A Final Report: Medical Response to Wife Abuse in Manitoba: A Survey of Physicians' Attitudes and Practices.* Winnipeg, MB: University of Manitoba, School of Social Work, Child and Family Services Research Group, 1988.

1253. Turnbull, Debi, and Marvin Brown. "Attitudes towards Homosexuality and Male and Female Reactions to Homosexual and Heterosexual Slides." *Canadian Journal of Behavioural Science* 9, no. 1 (1977): 68-80.

1254. Weg, Ruth B. *Sexuality in Later Years: Roles and Behaviors.* New York, NY: Academic Press, 1983.

1255. West, D. J. "Rape As Revenge." *New Society* 45, no. 834 (1978): 684-86.

1256. Yarmey, A. Daniel. "Attitudes and Sentencing for Sexual Assault As a Function of Age and Sex of Subjects." *Canadian Journal on Aging* 4 (Spring 1985): 20-28.

Descriptor Index